Praise for Southern Seminary

"SEM was family. SEM was a one on one with your instructors and professors while having horses in your backyard (a first for most) I knew what College I wanted to attend at a very early age an I never veered away. Two wonderful years of growth, education and equestrian experiences as a student turned into 11 years as a SEM faculty member as assistant stable manager and equine instructor and 5 years as resident director of Craton Hall. Over those 11 years I tried to give back to my students the knowledge and education I had acquired over the years but most importantly I tried to show them the beauty and love that surrounded them on top of that hill. Along with the love of our SEM surroundings came the love of the SEM barn and the horses. Going from student to faculty might have aged me but the friendship gained along the way I cherish to this day. Life- long friendships were developed from that little treasure on the hill in Buena Vista, Virginia. SEM will always have my heart."

— Carolyn Hedrick Williams
Southern Sem Graduate and Instructor

"Every so often, at the beginning of each semester I would see a student seated in front of me that I did not recognize. They would be from different major areas rather than merchandising. When I could later converse with them outside the classroom, they would say they recognized that the subject they were taking from me could be relative to their current interest or major. These were 'thinking and planning' students who were opting to supplement their major studies with additional 'useful' studies. Their class input kept me motivated to make the subject relative to each individual. I was, also, proud to be a part of the 1983 Nationals Competition held at Southern Seminary. I played a big part in the preparation on that horse event. Bernie Gaiser and Katherine Sanford did all the horse stuff and I handled all the hospitality. As I recall, I also worked at the 'table' for the actual competitions. Southern Seminary had a wonderful team and I was very proud of the riders."

— Frank White
Merchandising Department

Riders of the Seminary

Copyright © 2024 by Bonnie Feldstein

All rights reserved.

ISBN 978-1-62806-405-6 (print | paperback)

Library of Congress Control Number 2024904776

Published by Salt Water Media
29 Broad Street, Suite 104
Berlin, MD 21811
www.saltwatermedia.com

Interior images provide by the author and/or used with permission
Front cover image of school from a contributor with additional graphic work
Back cover image of Banner and RT courtesy of Carolyn Hedrick Williams

Riders of the Seminary

A Journal of Amazing American Women Equestrians

by

Bonnie Gillespie Feldstein '67

Dedication

To all riders who love their horses more than anything.

*"I heard them nickering in the night.
The barn was calling; I had to go."*

Contents

Introduction 13

In a Small Town Far, Far Away ... In Virginia 15

Dreams Can Come True 17

A Slightly Clinical Way to Look at This Wonderful Majestic Animal 21

A Salute to the Instructors and Directors of the Great Sem Riders 23

The Winds of Change: 1950s 27

Music Makes the World Go 'Round: 1960s 31

A Wild Ride in America: 1970s 37

Girls and Horses, Please Step Forward: 1980s 57

The End of an Era: 1990s 83

The Virginia Horse Center 88

It Takes a Sisterhood 90

"For everything, there is a season..." 92

Acknowledgements 93

In Memoriam 95

Services 96

Introduction

After writing my novel, "The Ladies of the Seminary," I knew deep down there would have to be another story. While the first was a novel loosely based on the shared experiences of four girls who were all roommates in the nineteen sixties at a private all-girls' school. Added to the mayhem, a cadre of interesting characters catapulted the story to its sometimes hysterical heights.

However, this is a completely different look at that junior college in Virginia. This one is a journal that takes us inside the lives of young women who went there to continue to ride and study about horses. Truly, this became the heart of the school which many of us were oblivious to being we were into different courses and not paying too much attention to the barn activities out back. Oh, we all had a few friends who rode, but many of us were unaware of how totally into horses they were. While many of us went for different reasons and courses, it was the equine program that drew these gals who wanted to do no more than ride, ride, ride. While riding was a mainstay on the campus, no one could imagine how big it was going to get and bring a luster to the school that would live on way past the school's existence. Yes, I had much to learn.

I was fortunate to link up with the right folks who could really help me understand this rather different world I was going to be living in for months, no years, going forward. I can never repay those that helped me to not only understand what riders do and what they go through to get to where they wanted to be, but to help me see the whole picture of the equestrian world. I was becoming and am today a great appreciator of the sport, the riders, and the horses that I have come to know.

In the nineteen eighties, the equine program was poised and ready to go to the next level. When Anne Mish, director of the Physical Education Department, brought a man named Russ Walther, from Mary Washington College to look around Southern Seminary, it was obvious that the riders and horses were about to take the stage and do some truly astounding things.

With Walther entrenched as Director of the Equestrian program and the wonderful Katha-

A Christmas Horse at Sem
Image courtesy of the author

rine Sanford directing all things barn, Sem was ready. Fame was about to come and come it did due to the many fabulous trainers, directors and forward-thinkers of the school. It would go on to win titles, ribbons, and national championships that no other school could attain for many years. It would bring excellence to the IHSA (Intercollegiate Horse Show Association) competitions and live on forever in their records.

Even though our school passed into history being known as Southern Seminary, it rose like a mythical Phoenix of ancient times to give the nation a group of women who would matter greatly in the equestrian world.

It must be added here that the people who bought the school, renamed it Southern University of Virginia and turned it into a co-ed campus and four-year school. The era of two-year schools was passing away. They have been gracious to all of us who return and go back up to the hill to relive our memories. They have been very welcoming and have created a room for us and our history in their library. It's well worth the time if you are anywhere nearby.

Today, our equine graduates are everywhere in America and in many different countries, still competing, performing, training, coaching, teaching, judging, breeding, and helping youth to become the next generation of great and well-known riders. That's a Sem rider's duty and our legacy.

Many of us look back now and are drawn to the great days and friends we made in a small school, atop a big hill, in a town in the gorgeous Shenandoah Valley looking up at the beautiful Blue Ridge Mountains.

It is with great pride, humility, and a few bruises and knee knocks along the way, that I write this journal that still carries on the traditions and customs of horses and all who came to love them. We stand together as a loving and lasting sisterhood who all salute you as our fabulous and dear *RIDERS OF THE SEMINARY*. God Bless You!

Bob Cacchione, IHSA Founder
Image from eSullivan, EQ Media

In a Small Town Far, Far Away ... In Virginia

In the eighteen hundreds, in the southwestern part of Virginia, at the foothills of the Blue Ridge Mountains, there was much excitement about the discovery of Iron Ore mines in a small, almost hamlet size, town named Buena Vista. The town leaders were out of ideas of how to make the town come alive again in a post-Civil War era. The mines were about to change all that and give new life to a town that was almost out of hope.

The bank in Buena Vista quickly organized an ambitious plan to build a hotel. Their vision was for a grand hotel to be built on the large hilltop as you enter the town. It was a gamble, but one they were willing to take. They knew when word got out about the ore in the mines, the town would become a beehive of visitors and investors with their families. All they needed to do was to find the right man to design and help build this showpiece that would attract the crowds.

When S.W. Foulks arrived with his ideas and a rough rendering, they were all impatiently waiting to see him and unveil what they hoped would be the centerpiece for the town and all who lived nearby.

They were not disappointed. He had brought them the very latest in hotel designs that were already being built in the north. He was a master of Renaissance and Queen Anne design that would fit perfectly on the sprawling acres on the hill.

When news got out about the hotel, people's hopes were lifted and work was just what was needed. Investors began to visit Buena Vista and the bankers were delighted to help them out. It would take time to finish the hotel but in the meantime, the iron ore mines were making people in the area very rich. Buena Vista was beginning to become a well-known small town in Virginia.

In 1890, the hotel was completed and ready to open. The people came in droves just to see the grandeur of this approximately two hundred room edifice that was replete with rounded towers and a grand ballroom with gilded mirrors that would reflect the finery of the ladies and gentlemen who would be staying there or visiting from a town close by. The hotel would keep the lovely and genteel traditions of southern hospitality with balls and other entertainments. It was truly a picture of the old south.

Bowling Green Seminary in Bowling Green, Virginia

A Look Back...

Sara Jane Murray (on the bottom)
who would later have a daughter,
Sharon Pettricione, who also went to Sem

1929

Sara Jane Murray 1942-1943
on the Main steps

Sara Jane Murray 1942-1943

Dreams Can Come True

In 1867, in another small town in Virginia, a very bright woman named Alice Chandler was beginning to get frustrated that she couldn't expand her school for young girls and offer them more of a advanced education. The Bowling Green School for Young Women was known for being a good school to send your daughter to so she could be more prepared for her female duties as she grew up. They stayed in the house that was sold to them and learned reading, music, sewing, and the dances of the time. Southern traditions were very important in Miss Alice's school. She believed in traditions because they shaped your life and gave you perspective of where you came from and prepared you for wherever you might go.

No matter the success of what Alice Chandler had accomplished, she yearned for a higher education to be taught, but right now, it didn't seem that door might ever be opened. Then one day, a man named Edgar Rowe visited her school. She listened intently to what he had to say about education and where he thought her school might expand and the possibilities and opportunities that would be within a young woman's reach fairly soon. Alice was extremely impressed with Dr. Rowe. He stayed in town and visited Miss Chandler several times and on the last day they met for tea, he offered to buy her school. He offered to relieve her burdensome debt in trying to keep the school afloat and even went so far as to ask her to stay on as principle of the private school. How could she refuse this most generous offer? She couldn't and the papers were signed within a day or two and for the first time in many years, she could feel relaxed without the worry of having to recruit more girls to sustain the budget. At this time, after the Civil War, finding enough families who wanted to pay for their daughter to attend a private school took some real horse trading. The mothers were always obliging but the fathers weren't so sure in these difficult times of reconstruction. Many of the sons had already gone off to the Virginia Military Institute or a private male school such as Washington and Lee.

Contented with his latest acquisition, Dr. Rowe went off to find a more suitable place to move the school he had just bought. He saw the need and he was pretty sure he could finance one if he found such a place. He had been advised to go up to Buena Vista and take a look at the hotel on the hill and see if there would be space for the small academy there. He thought they would love to rent out some of the unused rooms for the academy. He was aware the hotel

Dr. Edgar H. Rowe
First President of Southern Seminary
Image from the Seminary yearbook

Dr. Robert Lee Durham
Second President of Southern Seminary
Image from the Seminary yearbook

was struggling, due to the dwindling iron ore mines that had once driven the building of the hotel.

Not one to pass up a good financial opportunity he set his sights on Buena Vista. After walking the many acres on top of the hill and speaking to the bank that held the mortgage, he thought there was a real possibility to acquire some of it for Miss Chandler's and his school.

After meeting with some of the trustees of the bank, they thought his idea might just work and help them out of a collapsing economy in the town, now with the mines being drained daily of the precious ore that made that area a boom town. He drove a tough bargain and needed to have much done to the building after a fire had burned down much of their bakery in the kitchen. Repairs needed to be done and then he would sign all the necessary papers.

He returned to Bowling Green to tell Alice what he was up to and see if she agreed to the plan. She didn't just agree, she began to pack up the things the new place would need. Naturally, she would miss this school that she had worked so hard to establish, but the new home would give her students so many wonderful opportunities that she couldn't deny them.

By 1900 the school was good to go and they moved it into the Buena Vista Hotel. With the big boom of the iron ore mines now gone, they had the entire hotel to themselves. After everyone and everything was settled in, Dr. Rowe had a little celebration and renamed the school Southern Seminary College. A whole new era had begun for this beautiful building.

Not too long after the school was established in Buena Vista and word got out, Dr. Robert Lee Durham came to visit the school. He had been the Dean of Martha Washington College which had merged with Emory College. He was a man with some wealth and he offered to buy half of the school from Dr. Rowe, who was beginning to think about retirement. Dr. Durham was quite a catch for the school. He was an educator, administrator, author and inventor. However, the most important thing about Dr. Durham was that he brought new, higher standards of academic study and worked hard to get a high standard of accreditation to Southern Seminary. The enrollment grew rapidly and the word got out that Southern Seminary was quite the school to attend. With the proper footing established, the future of the small college was assured.

Along with Dr. Durham came his wife and his most precious daughter, Margaret. She loved their new home and loved the campus. It was an exciting time in life for her and her family. Margaret loved living on top of the huge hill and walking all the trails that were there. She made friends quickly with her winning personality. While her father and mother were very strict about house rules, Margaret became a most desirable, young southern lady. She exuded everything the school stood for and as she grew, Dr. Durham saw the potential she had for possibly taking a much larger role in the school.

People in small, southern towns, do a bit of polite "gossiping," and most of it concerns eligible young men and eligible young women, so naturally it wouldn't be long before Dr. Durham's lovely young daughter would catch the eye of some eligible men near the town. There was one in particular, however, who showed a great interest in Miss Margaret and after her father gave his approval, a handsome, young businessman from Buena Vista came to call. H. Russell Robey had an outgoing personality and was said to be quite a catch for any young woman who might draw his attention, and apparently Margaret Durham had done just that. They were both smitten after one date and they married in 1922. This would be the

H. Russell Robey
School Business Manager
Image from the Southern Seminary archives

beginning of a dynasty at Southern Seminary that would last for decades.

Russell was all he said about himself and he turned out to be a very good businessman who also had saved a good bit of money. He shared his visions with Margaret for moving forward with his desire to buy out the half of the school from Dr. Rowe and then the Durham/Robey families would have total ownership. Dr. Rowe, who had married Miss Chandler's sister years before was beginning to age and Miss Alice Chandler had moved back to her hometown in Georgia a while back, so it seemed a good time to present Rowe with his idea. When he sat down and made the offer, Dr. Rowe was frankly very happy to take him up on his plan.

Mr. Robey now owned Rowe's share and everyone seemed happy with the arrangement.

After the deal was legally complete, the family agreed that Margaret should become the second president of the school, giving her sole judgment on the academics of the school. Russell Robey would be named the Business Director.

Margaret Robey and H. Russell Robey in 1929
Image from the Southern Seminary archives

Maragret Durham Robey
President of Southern Seminary (1967)
Image from the 1967 Seminary yearbook

Russell's vision of the school was now complete and he knew Margaret would be wonderful giving the young women a solid education while he brought not only his business acumen but his passion and love of horses.

According to the archives, horses had always been a large pastime of the Virginia culture and in the early years of the school riding was enjoyed by small groups of women while they were at Southern Seminary. But Mr. Robey had dreams of what he wanted to do with the riding program. He was going to expand it and allow the girls who were going to attend the school, an invitation to bring their own horses, if they chose to do so. It was made clear there would be extra costs for their stabling and care, and the girls were expected to participate without question in the mucking of stalls, care of their animals, and care of the barn.

He decided he would seek to buy or have donated to the school suitable horses for the girls who didn't bring their own, so all who wanted could participate in riding for physical education as well as show and hunt. He loved this part of his job and was ready to go when a call came in to him that a horse might be available. Russell became an excellent horse buyer and the girls loved that he took such a keen interest in their riding and show activities. It soon became second nature for the girls to be in the barn for many hours doing what was expected, and doing so many other things that brought the equestrian gals into being a very tight-knit group of students.

Little did he know that his passion would become the passion of many of the girls who would come to the school because they had a small equine program. And no one could see that one day that equine program would grow and grow and be recognized nationally.

A Slightly Clinical Way To Look at This Wonderful Majestic Animal

No one really knows for sure when the horse was present on earth. But we do know it was always here with humans. Many cave paintings told the story of the horse and man and many had to do with the horse helping the man either in very early agriculture or in war. The horse was a protector of our species and stood side by side us all the way through our known history and probably long before man. No matter, truth be told the story and history of the ancients and horses dated well before anything we are certain of.

This magnificent animal was encountered in the wild, running with its mane flying in the wind. No more incredible sight is known. No doubt man was in awe and a little afraid of this wild creature because the horse is strong and tall and can be hostile if the adventurer tries to tame it way before it's practicable.

The sheer strength of a horse can easily be seen in its legs and mid-section, muscular beyond belief. The horse's body is a masterpiece of beauty and the human and the horse are made to be together, but make no mistake, one must respect the horse. Not to do so is at one's own peril. When a horse is angry the kick can do real damage and cause permanent injuries. Plus, any rider can tell you with absolute honesty that horses can give you a mean bite. So, beware when approaching in haste.

To capture the horse's anatomy, these charts should give you a good idea of what's where and where the real strength of the horse comes from. They are truly remarkable animals!

Lisa Shelton '88 and Honta
"True Love"

Image from a contributor

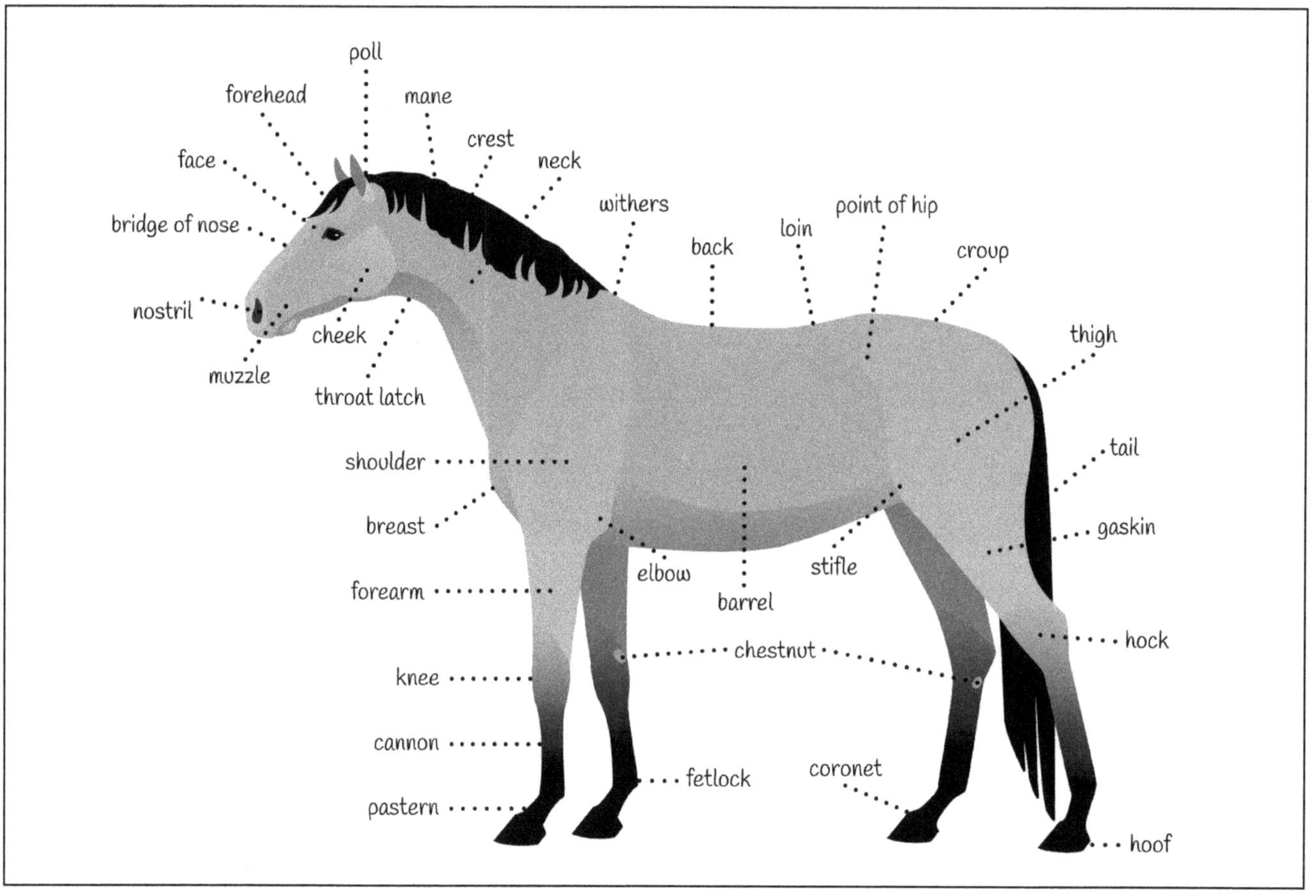

Horse External Anatomy

- poll
- forehead
- mane
- face
- crest
- neck
- bridge of nose
- withers
- back
- loin
- point of hip
- croup
- nostril
- cheek
- muzzle
- throat latch
- thigh
- tail
- shoulder
- gaskin
- breast
- stifle
- forearm
- elbow
- barrel
- hock
- chestnut
- knee
- cannon
- coronet
- pastern
- fetlock
- hoof

Horse Skeletal Anatomy

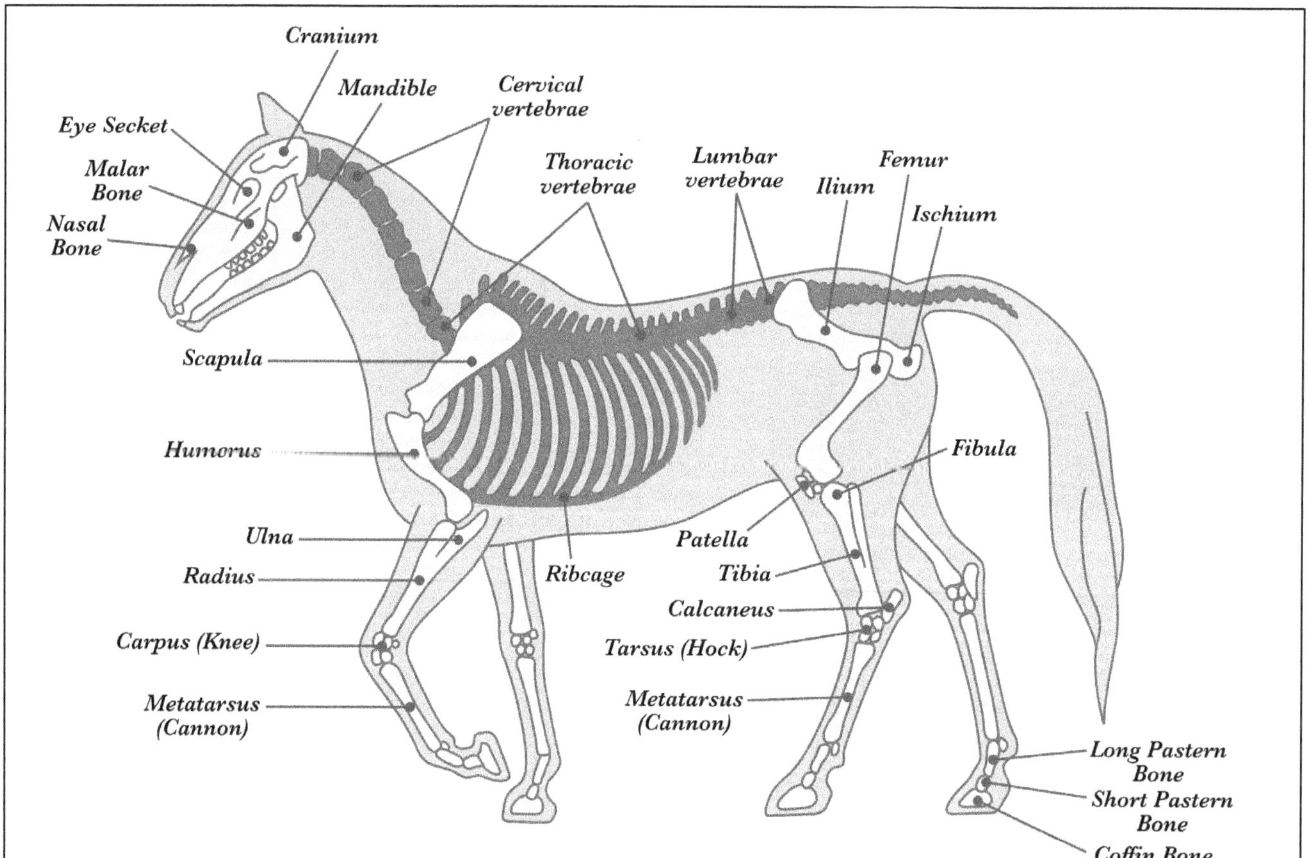

- Cranium
- Mandible
- Cervical vertebrae
- Eye Socket
- Thoracic vertebrae
- Lumbar vertebrae
- Femur
- Malar Bone
- Ilium
- Ischium
- Nasal Bone
- Scapula
- Humerus
- Fibula
- Ulna
- Patella
- Radius
- Ribcage
- Tibia
- Calcaneus
- Carpus (Knee)
- Tarsus (Hock)
- Metatarsus (Cannon)
- Metatarsus (Cannon)
- Long Pastern Bone
- Short Pastern Bone
- Coffin Bone

A Salute to the Instructors and Directors of the Great Sem Riders

Anne Mish – our ever-faithful Director of Physical Education

Cecil Stanford – Director/Instructor of Equitation through the 60s

Katharine Sanford Connor – Instructor and Barn Manager

Bernie Gaiser – Director/Instructor of Equitation from the 60s on

Kevin Irwin – Instructor

* **Patti Carroll** – Instructor

Carl Bessette – Director/Instructor

* **Leslie Brown** – Instructor

* **Liz Courter** – Instructor

David Damewood – Instructor

Hugh White – Instructor

* **Carolyn Hedrick** – Instructor

Russ Walther – Director/Instructor and Directed Sem in the "Golden Years of the Eighties and was recently inducted into the IHSA (Intercollegiate Horse Show Association) Hall of Fame

Pam Doe – Instructor

JT Tallon – Instructor who became Director when Russ left

Chris Wynn – Instructor

* **Kim Diehl DeBonte** – Instructor

Thom Pollard – Director/Instructor

Julie Lake – Barn Manager

Sarah Irvine – Instructor

Amy Reistrup – Instructor

* **Cindy Judson Kelley** – Barn Manager

Sandy Gerald – Director when Thom Pollard left

*Indicates Sem Alums

*Left to right:
JT Tallon, Carolyn Hedrick Williams, Trainer, and Katharine Sanford, Barn Manager
Image from the Seminary yearbook*

Anne Mish,
Director of the Physical Education Program

Image from the Seminary yearbook

JT Tallon
Director of Equine Program

Image from the Seminary yearbook

Bernard W. Gaiser, Director, and Katharine Sanford, Barn Manager

Image from the Seminary yearbook

Russ Walther
Director of the Equine Program
Image from the Seminary yearbook

David Damewood
Trainer
Image from the Seminary yearbook

Bob Cacchione
Intercollegiate Horse Show Association Founder
*Image courtesy of Holly Hill Wallace
at the 2023 Reunion at Ocala*

Pam Doe
Trainer
Image from the Seminary yearbook

Hugh White
Trainer
Image from the Seminary yearbook

Coach Amy Reistrup, Director, (left) with
Missie Morrissey '92 after winning
Cacchione Cup in Zone 4
Image from the Seminary yearbook

Cecil Stanford
Director of Equine Program (1950s and 1960s)
Image from the Seminary yearbook

The Winds of Change: 1950s

The winds of change had arrived. WWII was over and people wanted to get on with life and were hopeful of new times that would bring new opportunities. America was ready to try to put the past behind and their feelings were that there was work to be done and money to be made. They were ready to have some fun as well.

The era of Big Band music which came to signify a war-time period was giving way to a new and more raucous sort of expression. This music was targeted more to the young with a nod to a very different kind of tune. It was more capricious and definitely louder, a challenge for the older crowd who loved their bands and romantic melodies.

The age of "Rock 'n' Roll" had arrived. Names like The Big Bopper, Richie Valens, and Buddy Holly (to name a few) including the KING - Elvis Presley who had already entered the fray in the later 50s, would take center stage. The Big Bopper, Valens, and Holly would gain great fame but tragically be killed together in a plane crash that would stagger the hearts and minds of the young. Later, at the end of the 60s, Don McLean who write a song named, "The Day The Music Died" and was also called "American Pie" but wouldn't be released until 1971. It was inspired by the airplane crash that took the life of Buddy Holly and the other two men. The song was so popular that it immortalized all three for years to come, even to today. Its considered a classic for all times.

It wasn't long before a mysterious man in black came along by the name of Johnny Cash and country music would raise its head and bring new names to the music scene and a new way of singing about heartbreak and disappointment between a man and a woman. Great stars of this time in Country Music were: Patsy Cline, Hank Williams, Chet Atkins to name a few. They were the beginning of a huge business. These singers were beloved by the rural country folks who adored the sound of their steel guitars and twanging voices. At the time, no one could imagine that country music would become mainstream music and loved by most in the country today. However, to the middle class of the fifties, country music, motorcycles, guitars and twanging voices, were not in the mainstream or preference to the monied society that was growing by leaps and bounds.

While the youth was boppin' to the tunes and going to "sock hops," the parents were working hard and moving to the suburbs in greater and greater numbers. Life was changing rapidly in the country and so were the ideals of going away to a college for a higher education. That was the goal of most of the middle class, and it would stay that way for decades to come.

Teens were beginning to explore their sexuality in a different, less Victorian way and question some of the standards by which you were judged innocent. For better or worse, authors were writing books for this age group encouraging them to question the standards of the past. A new word was appearing in the culture for young, and older women that would change everything as time moved forward. Once the genie was released from the bottle by Betty Friedan, "Feminism" would begin to take root in the culture and it would cause an uproar. It was certainly a game-changer for both men and women. However, at Southern Seminary at this time, old traditions and ways were kept and young ladies were still expected to honor the old ways. There were fairly strict rules and they were to be kept if you were to stay at school. So, as the world continued on, for many of us, things were still the same as they had always been.

However, nothing stays beautiful and smooth. Once again, the winds were blowing in the direction of another war. Young men would go off to a new and different kind of war. One where you drew a line and couldn't cross over it. It would be in a far-off place called Korea. This line, known as a DMZ (Demilitarized Zone) would lead to frustration because no one would conclusively win the war and, at the end, caused the country to separate into two different countries: North and South Korea. Many American men died over there and it would signal a new kind of warfare. One that wasn't at all like WWII.

By the time Korea was over and things began to settle back into a routine, most mothers in the middle class stayed home. Many were glad to get away from the factory work for the war effort. They had grown accustomed to being home and with their children when they

Nancy Ginavan '59 - The Saddle Club with trainer/coach Cecil Stanford

Image from the Seminary yearbook

Nancy Ginavan '59 - The Trail Club

Image from the Seminary yearbook

got home from school. There were so many improved home products to make lives easier and better. Appliances of convenience were flooding the country and they made the woman's life much easier and gave her more time for social things like volunteering and travel. A new game was sweeping the middle class. Bridge was becoming an obsession to many women who formed "Bridge Clubs" and invited women to their homes. On weekends many couples found that a great, social entertainment. I will bet anything that many of you remember coming home after school when the Bridge Club was there and being ushered straight out of the living room or wherever the Bridge tables were set up. But, the flipside of that is we learned how to play the game and I can close my eyes and still smell the smoke from the large and small smokers at Sem and watch all the girls playing Bridge. There seemed to be an invisible divide between the smokers. Large one was for freshman and the small one was for the senior girls. It seemed to me if you were a freshman and you wanted to go into the small smoker, you needed to be "invited" in, so the object was to make a good friend who was a senior. Then we could go in there and play Bridge with the "upper" class girls. Weren't we something?

Bigger stoves and refrigerators were a tremendous hit. Snacks and nibbles were coming along by the hundreds which would prove to be a disaster to a weight problem later on. Something called "TV Dinners" were being used to feed the kids when parents went out for the night and would later on become a quick and easy dinner for everyone.

Tampons were a real game-changer when they came along to replace sanitary pads with those awful sanitary belts that were so uncomfortable and I don't care what anyone said, you could see that bump in the back of your skirt or dungarees. Yes, I said Dungarees.

For now, kids had a carefree life to do what they pleased. It was a time of peace and freedom.

The fifties, many or most would say, was the best of times. What would follow would be anyone's guess, but for now, it was a blast to be young and "Do-Wop-Diddy Diddying" along.

The brilliant riders at Southern Seminary were beginning to really make headway and competitions were being won in the shows with great regularity. The school was beginning to become a college where women could ride and take a keener interest in equine studies.

Mr. Robey had always been a horse lover and his dream was to make the equitation program truly excellent. Often, he would find horses around the county and people would donate them to the school for the girls to ride. As the Business Director, he wanted to make the program grow much larger so he would invest in the program so it would have all tools and accommodations the girls needed to make the program grow. Directors Anne Mish and Cecil Stanford were there to provide the necessary advice to grow the physical Education department Mr. Robey had a plan and knew that one day that plan would pay off. For now, though, it was still about practice, learning and local shows. The girls delighted in entertaining the parents when they came to their graduation weekends. The lower ring was transformed into a beehive of activity with refreshments served. Traditions were becoming legend to the girls and the school.

Nancy Ginavan '59

Image courtesy of her daughter and Sem rider Tammy Ginavan '88

*From the 1957 Yearbook:
Paddock and Along the Trail
May Fete and Dance*
Image from the Seminary yearbook

One of them was the Horses's Christmas Tree. I mean how wonderful is that? To watch the girls coming in a line on their horses, dressed in formal riding habits, to the tree to have horsey snacks and their pictures taken. In later years they dressed the horses up for their Christmas party and the tree ceremony where riders would lead the horse close enough to the tree to gently nibble off a carrot or an apple. It was truly something wonderful to watch. And there was always a Santa to visit. Mostly that was one of the girls who would enter on horseback as if she was in that sleigh in the Macy's Day Parade. Town folks came from all around to enjoy the festivities and usually one of the local papers would be sure to send a reporter to record the holiday happenings on campus. It was quite a thing at Sem. No one could ever say we didn't love and admire our riders and their most beloved horses, whether they were their own or one of the school's horses. We were all proud to be a part of such a fabulous school.

Sem was enjoying a solid student body with so much more to come. Many people look back at the fifties and remark wistfully, "It was the best of times."

*A photo of the Southern Seminary
Students Handbook from the early 1940s*
Image from a Seminary alumna

Music Makes the World Go 'Round: 1960s

And just like that, the world seemed to change overnight. The good times kept on rolling and we were in high school with so many things to think about. The President was John F. Kennedy and his wife, Jackie, would usher us into a new fashion world. The Pill-Box hat, designed by Halston, was a stunner and we all simply HAD to have one. Not one young girl looked awful in that hat. It was incredibly chic. Jacqueline taught us what fashion really was all about. We were always "ladies," but Mrs. Kennedy took us on a fashion ride we would never forget. When she and the President held a White House Dinner, we couldn't wait to see what Jackie wore. I often wonder if the President got jealous of how much we loved her?

This was the decade of our dreams. Our mothers, fathers, aunts and uncles, had come through the Depression and then a World War with pictures that would shock the entire world when, what became known as the Holocaust, was uncovered and we learned six million Jewish people were exterminated systematically.

Life magazine photographers recorded this unspeakable tragedy in detail and we saw what true evil looked like. The pictures came in from the Asian Theater of the horrors of Corregador, and Battan, and talk of forced marches would never leave our minds. The photo of our incredible Marines holding up our American Flag at Iwo Jima would become an internal battle cry for patriotism and courage.

With all that, we were still young and carefree. We didn't spend too much time on the past, but, respectfully, listened to our elders who were recording those moments in history upon our hearts so we would remember.

Southern Seminary Junior College was making some bold initiatives in the world of colleges to attract young women who wanted to ride and gain education about equine business so they could go out of school and work in the horse industry. They began advertising in teen and equine magazines. I remember the ads back then and they always had horses in the background and they all seemed to be going off to the hunt, in beautiful riding attire, surrounded by their wonderful hounds. The school ads stayed in my sub-conscious mind and as my brothers went off to college, I was finally the only kid at home. I had time now to discover other things and one of those things was BOYS. And I learned that boys my age always had one thing on their minds, and that the girls my age had that same thing on their minds. Oh, for those days of innocence and going to the movies to come back now. We had dances they called "open houses" where we could go try out one or two of the new dances with music that encouraged outrageous dance styles. The mash potato, the stroll, the twist, and always the most loved "slow dance." Oh yes, those were the ones we enjoyed most if the boy we had a crush on would ask us to dance. Totally nerdy now a days. Then, something extraordinary happened to us in the sixties. "The British Invasion" came to America. We met the Beatles – John, George, Paul and a mop – headed drummer named Ringo. Who will ever forget "I Want To Hold Your Hand?" I know my father would never get that song out of his head as he drove us to school every morning with the Number One hit playing on the Herb Oscar Anderson Show out of New York City. Our dear parents were trapped in a time warp and they just couldn't understand our way of talking, being hipsters, cool cats and listening to groups such as The Beatles, The Rolling Stones, and then there was the Motown sound coming along and we adored The Supremes and dozens of others. There were many, many changes in music and so many great groups for us to sing and dance along with tunes we still know today. Who can forget the lyrics to those classical rock and roll songs? It was a time of ridiculous songs like Alley Oop, and Little Nash Rambler, and on and on. Such good memories. We were the generation of change. And it would effect everything around us.

We all had transistor radios to listen to and all the new inventions coming along for young women were fantastic. We were still rolling our hair up every night and sometimes with toilet paper rolls. Incredible stuff. Panty Hose would come to take the place of nylons and garter belts that dug into our thighs that we would never forget. Ban Roll-On deodorant was a hit and so were foam rollers which always seemed to leave a rut in our hair but they were kinder and gentler to us than the wire rollers most of us would still sleep in with a scarf to cover them.

When we traveled, we used to those encased hair dryers with a long plastic tube that blew the hot air through plastic tubes to dry our hair. Unbelievable in today's world, but back then, we were so "far out."

As time came for us to choose a college to attend, we had so many choices, but those ads for Southern Seminary kept ringing in our heads. Dads took us to a slew of other schools to interview, but when we went down to a small town named Buena Vista in Virginia, I fell in love with that big red main building. I spoke to a few folks and can remember on the way home praying I would get in. I know you all have memories that are similar. For you riders, I should think it wasn't a hard choice at all. By the sixties, ribbons and trophies were filling the champion cases in Main and the barn was a beehive of activity. You had entered horse heaven.

I don't know about you, but from the time I got my acceptance to the day I arrived, I never had second thoughts. I was certain. Through

Frank White
Merchandising Director (1966 and onward)
Image from the Seminary yearbook

high school I worked hard inside and out around NYC in the wonderful world of opera and then Broadway music. By the time I was seventeen, I was ready to do something different and get away from the big city and go to a smaller, quieter place. I had no idea what lay ahead of me, but I knew it would be fantastic. What I didn't imagine is that this new adventure in a small, southern town would be wonderful and interesting in a way I never thought it could be. And finding out there was not one, but two, all male colleges six miles away, sealed the deal. Wow!

By the end of the sixties, Sem was consistently winning championships in riding- both in show, jumping and going off to the hunts in Rockbridge County. Merchandising became a huge draw for the school with the addition of Mr. Frank White who came in '67 and all I can say, lovingly that is the school would NEVER be the same again. He was the most talented man in his field and there isn't one girl who took courses from him who would ever forget him. He even effected the girls who were riders who would one day graduate and then go out and work on horse farms or have farms themselves. He was an amazing professor.

Anne Mish was an essential employee at Southern Seminary for many years. She was head of the Physical Education program and the equestrian program. A superb woman who had a profound effect on any and all the students who worked with her.

Cecil Stanford, the riding Director, was an integral part of the riding program in these early years of growth for equine students. Between Anne Mish and Cecil Stanford, the program took on new aspects while still performing and winning in hunts and shows. Sem was becoming the team to beat among other colleges that offered competition riding.

A very dsad note here is that the 1960s would bring our nation much sorrow with the war in Vietnam, a war that would last until the late 70s. The girls who dated and married VMI cadets would feel the sorrow greatly. It seemed these decades of teh 40s, 50s, 60s, and onward would continue to witness the sting of war and its horros that left such wounds on our hearts.

Joan Hallford Abernathy '66

Joan was a beautiful rider who was a member of both The Saddle Club (A campus club that was well-regarded by the Sem horse riders. You had to be an advanced and well-trained rider to be included.) Joan was also a member of the Equitation Club, a school club that had been around since the beginning of the program. This club was for the girls who rode at all levels.

Her instructor was Cecil Stanford.

She came to Sem from Iran. Her father was

Joan Hallford '66
Image from of the Seminary yearbook

in military service there. She was a talented rider, and her horses were sent to Sem on a steamer ship not by air, to be sure they arrived safely. "One of them, however, was quite shaken," she says, "But upon arrival but did make a good recovery."

Joan was involved in school the judicial council and served as student president, which she was very proud to do. She was fortunate to find her life mate at VMI: Jan Abernathy) and ther were married after they're schooling was completed.

Today, Joan is writing a book that she hopes to have published soon. It's about being a young American girl growing up in Iran. She is joined in that literary passion with her husband, who is also writing a book. So, stay tuned for the Abernathy books.

Her Recollections:

"I loved Sem and flourished there, participating in all things horse, as well as my studies. I was proud to ride my one horse, 'Persian Lady,' a magnificent looking horse who made me feel so regal when riding on her."

Sharon Petriccione Angelo '67

Sharon's memories are a bit different when it comes to riding. She went to Sem as a "Kin Club member." Her mother, Sara Jane Murray, went to Sem in the 1940s and she was a rider. Sharon did not ride at the school, but funny/sentimental story is that while Sharon did not ride at Sem, she had ridden before she went there and then afterwards. She was even in some local shows back near her home in York, Pennsylvania. Go figure that one, but the interesting fact here is, that while communicating her story she shared that while she didn't ride at Sem — she was too busy with her other studies — she told me that she kept her mother's riding

Sharon Petriccione '67
at a horse show in Pennsylvania.

Image courtesy of Sharon Petriccione Angelo '67

boots from her years riding at Sem. They were a precious memory of years gone by. When they finally wore out, she had to dispose of them. We can all imagine how that sad day went.

Grace Adele Franzrep Hall '67

Grace arrived at Sem in a flurry. She was always a gal who was larger than life and we loved her spirit. Never without a smile on her face, she embodied the essence of a "Typical Southern Seminary Woman."

Coming from a family who had horses and trained them for the movies and entertainment industry, she was a super rider upon arrival. She understood the horse and proved that while riding at Sem.

She was a member of the Saddle Club.

Her instructor was Cecil Stanford, who had been at Sem for a while and was there through the sixties and stayed a little while into the seventies until Bernie Gaiser came along and became the Director.

She was Mistress of ceremonies for the Christmas Tree parade, leading the way. Seeing her on her gorgeous black steed, with full

Grace Franzrep '67
Image from the Seminary yearbook

Karen "Jill" Kennedy '68 with Comet of Lazy J
Image courtesy of Karen "Jill" Kennedy

riding habit and magnificent hat, she was truly a grand representative of the Equitation program at Sem.

In the 1967 yearbook, Grace is quoted giving one of the best equine blessings around for riders everywhere. "May you never die 'til a dead horse kicks you!" Thanks, Grace.

Grace still rides and hunts in Virginia.

She lives in Susan, Virginia and she and her husband are well-known for their 4th of July parade. Maybe we should visit her one of these days.

Karen "Jill" Kennedy '68

"Sem was a great experience for me."

While Jill wasn't a show rider or a hunter while at Sem, she used her experience and all she learned at school for later in life after graduation. Riding the school horses was her passion and she was given the opportunity with her roommate and Mr. Robey to buy two new horses for the program: They ended up becoming remarkable school favorites Banner and RT, whose real name was Rigorous Training, but the girls fondly nicknamed him "Rat Turd."

Her instructor was Cecil Stanford and she loved Ann Mish.

Her best friend while at Sem was Beverly Green who was a very talented rider with great promise, but was killed later on. A vet sad time for Jill.

Jill became a factory rep and at one time worked for Haliburton Industries. She traveled a lot.

She is a member of APHA and PIHA. She loves the Pintos and Paints and has won many comptitions with them.

"Horses are my passion, not my business," she says.

However, you can see how much time she has devoted to her passion, winning over a thousand belt buckles in her competitions as well as many trophies.

While at Sem she was proud the day of her graduation when her father was guest speaker and gave the graduation speech.

1966 Equitation Club
Image from the Seminary yearbook

Author's Note: Some of the wonderful friends of this author who were at Sem in the 60s and who were wonderful riders, but I have lost track of over the years. I mention them below:

Margaret (Peggy) Daly
Patricia Perry
Lillian Burkett
Charlotte (Charl) Passapae

These are but a few of the super riders. The program was still growing, but these girls and many more went out on hunts at Rockbridge Hunt Club and won a ton of ribbons and trophies. I am sure a good portion of them, like Grace Franzrep, still ride and enjoy the memories they made at Sem.

A Wild Ride in America: 1970s

The Seventies were marked by bellbottoms, war movies, and protests. The protests were now beginning to get out of hand on most college campuses and there were anti-war protests and some that even went so far as to deteriorate into riots. Southern Seminary wasn't as affected as many of the other campuses perhaps because it was a small campus with a small student body and this would have truly had a deep effect on the school and its culture. Plus the fact that a major military school (Virginia Military Institute) was a few miles away and many of the girls dated (and married) many of the cadets and saw how upsetting this war was to them due to the fact that many would be going overseas to fight right after graduation.

All the decades before the late 60s and afterwards would be noted as "the best of times in America," but the country changed during and after that war. It became a country torn in two, separating parents from children and pitting friends against one another. Families would fight over it and some youth would run away rather than fight in Vietnam. The government was divided as well and it seemed the country would never laugh again or come together in a meaningful way. Old traditions and customs were giving way to a more open society.

Noticeable fashion trends marked this new society with wild patterns and new fabrics such as polyester. Students in colleges no longer wanted the old ways of doing things and many traditions were giving way.

With all the change going on, teachers were adjusting as well, but Southern Seminary held the line with many of its old traditions. Sometimes it seemed as if time stood still on that hill in Buena Vista, and maybe it did, which wasn't so bad either. Merchandising, Equitation, and Kindergarten teacher training were still the major courses that drew young women to the school. All I can say is thank heavens horses don't change nor do the riders who adore them. Even the riding habits remained the same (and still do, pretty much).

The world was engulfed in politics. Watergate would come to signify corruption at the highest level. President Richard Nixon resigned in disgrace and his administration was severely punished. Several went to prison.

Drugs became a national phenomenon

afflicting the middle class. Celebrity overdoses were beginning to happen at an alarming rate. Many of the soldiers returning from Vietnam were using drugs to help them with their PTSD. Singing greats such as Janis Joplin, Jimi Hendrix, and Jim Morrison would die and keep headlines burning with this new plague. Drugs were now on their way to a new kind of war for us and our young.

We laughed at Archie Bunker's craziness and outspoken commentary in the hit TV series *All in the Family* as eighteen-year-olds won their right to vote.

1973 the high court voted to make *Roe V. Wade* the law of the land which would set us on the path to a long and continuous battle over abortion.

The Viet Nam Peace Accords began in Paris in hopes of ending the Vietnam War, which was tearing our country apart with dissention and violent protests.

1975 Gerald Ford changed his title from Vice President to President after the Nixon resignation.

Finally in 1975, the VIETNAM WAR WAS OVER! The effects of that war would go on and on for decades and see soldier deaths escalate from Agent Orange exposure and other injuries sustained in that war. Today, in 2023, we still suffer from those horrible effects of a war most wanted forgotten, but we salute our brave men and women who went over there and fought in the jungles and fields of Vietnam.

1976 brought us a new president - James Earl Carter, better known as Jimmy Carter. In hindsight, some call him our worst president due to a horrible economy and runaway inflation with high gas prices and long lines to get the gas.

Other notable things in the 70s would be:

- The death of Elvis Presley, who left millions of fans grieving, but making him a legend for all time.
- Atari enters as a new game system.
- First primitive computer enters the public marketplace that will change America and the world forever.
- VW "Bug" becomes a national favorite as a car.
- With high inflation and gas rationing along with long lines, many would come to say that these were quite possibly the worst of times.
- Jimmy Carter, who had become a very unpopular President would face a harsh election which he lost, as we zoom our way into the 80s.

The seventies were an odd time for our country and it surely brought the first big social changes at Southern Seminary. Some of the older more rigid rules were changing up to be more modern thinking for the times.

Girls coming to Sem were bringing their own cars for a few years but now many naturally brought them. They were also seeking more advanced courses so they could go on to four-year colleges. Two-year colleges were beginning to lose favor as the girls were moving on after Sem to four-year schools. The culture was changing and Southern Sem was forced to begin thinking in more modern terms for fear of what might become of the school if it didn't adjust.

Mr. Robey was convinced that the riding program was one answer to their dilemma. He knew there would always be a need for a college with higher education for the young women who wanted to ride and learn more about the business side of equitation. The school had hired a cadre of excellent instructors and the riding program was on its way to becoming tops in the regional and national shows. Names of some of the instructors who came in the seventies were: Bernie Gaiser, Scott Harris, Hugh White, Pam Doe, and David Damewood to mention a few. Katharine Sanford Connor remained the barn manager and she stayed on for many years.

Under the direction of these equine people, the riding program was shaping up to be incredible. Sem was now established as a major school for equestrian arts. The vision of Mr. Robey was coming to pass as he continued to receive some really fine horses.

Deborah Mapp Deschino '71
Image from the Seminary yearbook

Thumper, a beloved neighborhood dog who often visited the campus.
Image courtesy of Carolyn Williams

It should be noted here that a dog name "Thumper" roamed the campus and became best friend to many of the girls. She was most beloved by the girls.

Deborah Mapp Deschino '71

Deborah was in the Kindergarten Education program but she rode as well.

RT was the horse she rode while at Sem. She said, "He bucked, kicked, and bolted. When he came off the van, he would fly like the wind until he settled down."

Her instructor was Cecil Standford and then Katherine Sanford.

She rode with the Rockbridge Hunt every week and received many "colors" of which she was proud.

After Sem, Debbie worked with a space company named Airlock. They made space suit accessories. There was a fellow co-worker who loved race horses, so he and Debbie got involved with those horses.

She would break them in and train them for the starting gate. The horses raced at Aqueduct in New York.

Today Debbie lives in Connecticut and still rides horses occasionally. While she doesn't have any or her own, she says she wants to.

Nancy Dawn Ashway Webster '70-'73

Nancy had a good deal to say about Sem and, like the rest of us, she loved it. She was one of the first third-year students to return to Sem for added equine classes with Ann Mish. Her good friend, Patti Carroll, joined her in doing the same. She lived in Lexington because, at the time, the third-year house wasn't available. Later a house was devoted to girls wanting to return for a third semester for these classes. For the girls who stayed on, it gave each of them opportunities they needed to advance in their equine pursuits.

She studied with Ann Mish and Cecil Stanford. Later that year, Katharine Sanford joined the Sem riding team as a trainer. Nancy bought a horse from Ann Mish named Mad Tally. She trained on him and rode to the Rockbridge Hunt with him. He was wonderful horse who also joined in the fun with her for the annual horses' Christmas tree parade. There were other times when she would go out to Goshen and hang out and have picnics and ride trails out there. Goshen was a beautiful place that was adored by all the girls who went out there.

Patti Carroll was her close friend at Sem and she also stayed on for the third-year program as well.

It was during this time that the Board of Southern Seminary began talking about what to do with the old barn. It desperately needed repairs, but that was going to cost a good deal of money that the school wasn't prepared to spend at the time. They began to think about fundraising to see what they could bring in to make this happen, but the fundraising and planning wouldn't come for another decade.

Life After Sem:

Nancy judges for the US Equestrian and Maryland Horse Show Association.

Today Nancy has a lovely farm (Country Comfort Farm) on Maryland's Eastern Shore and she is the owner/trainer. Her farm has lessons, boarding, and indoor ring. She still professionally judges.

Nancy is married to David Webster.

Patti Carroll '72-'73

Patti's first words were, "Sem was the best time of my life." A sentiment that was held by most of the girls who went there. Didn't matter where you came from, the Sem Sisters all loved the school.

Her instructor was Bernie Gaiser and the horse she rode was none other than one of the school's favorites, RT, who she said taught her confidence and how to be bold when she rode.

"He could be a real stinker when you first approached him in his stall, but once you got his blanket on, he knew you meant business."

Ann Mish explained him to all of as a little horse with a large stride." Patti said, "I learned quickly what she meant. In fact when we went out to the ring, and get ready to jump over the fence he would actually leave out one or so

Patti Carroll '71 on RT
Image courtesy of Patti Carroll

Patti Carroll '71 on RT at the Equitation Championship in 1971 with Iris McNeil judging

Image from a contributor

strides and I had to get used to that and them try to make up for it."

"As riders, you have to go through everything. The good, the bad, and definitely the ugly. We were survivors, really. We saw blood and guts and we had to deal with trailers that wouldn't always cooperate, but we learned to get it done. We had no choice, we had to if we were going to ride.

"Back then, IHSA wasn't yet at Sem. That came later on, but we went to Sweetbriar and they had a grand indoor ring. We loved it. However, we really had to work hard and be serious in order to beat them, but we did! We rode against Hollins and Randolph Macon. We knew we could win, so we did. Eventually, we beat them all. Not every time, but enough to give us some neat bragging rights.

"Sem taught me everything from the ground up. It was that way for many of the girls who went to Sem. Today, I find the riders don't know much about the business of the horse - we did! We knew what it took to get on that magnificent animal and make them ride with us as a pair, not a solo act. Sem had some of the best instructors anywhere around in the country. We were fortunate," Patti remembered.

After school, Patti stayed around and taught beginners with Bernie. She loved doing that. "After I left Sem, I jumped in Virginia. Mostly amateur shows in hunter/jumper and was the champion of all I jumped in. and won Jr. Championships with the HQHA. I had a boarding farm for a while with my father until he died in '79. After horses, I became a Health Care aide up until I retired. Today I enjoy my life in a small town in Connecticut," Patti said.

One more important note: "Katherine Sanford really cared for those horses and took many of them when they needed to be helped or to keep until they died. RT was one of those horses, and so was Banner - the two most beloved horses at Southern Seminary. They lived out their lives under the watchful care Miss Sanford gave them and when they passed, she buried them with the dignity and love they deserved."

Stephanie Ann Head Jeffords '73

Her nickname was "Tipper" and her instructor was Bernie Gaiser. She was the Captain of the Sem Horse Drill Team which performed on special occasions. Fox hunting at Rockbridge Hunt was where she and her horse, Soldier Blue, like to go on weekends. Stephanie participated in every sport at Sem and at graduation received the highly-coveted Sem "Athletic Jacket."

She was one of only two girls from Oklahoma at Sem. She remembers that most of the girl were from the east coast.

One of her achievements was in receiving a Master's Certificate. That was like gold and highly respected by other riders and instructors.

Life After Sem:

Stephanie competed at the Harrisburg Horse Show and rode against Rodney Jenkins

Stephanie Head Jeffords '73
Sem Championship Lower Ring
Image from a contributor

Stephanie Jeffords '73 on Soldier Blue at the Harrisburg Competition in 1973
Image from a contributor

who was an outstanding and well-known at the time in riding circles. "I placed 4th which was phenomenal. People there were so impressed with my riding that they asked me to try out for our Olympic Riding Team," she said. Stephanie was thrilled because this was the dream, but later on, she had to decline due to unfortunate family issues.

After graduation and OCS, Stephanie joined the US Army and served for 30 years. During that time, her last service was a 10-year stint at the Pentagon. Today, she is in the Army Museum at Fort Belvoir, Virginia.

Stephanie has a fascinating background. She is half-Cherokee of the Chickamauga Cherokee Nation and speaks the native language.

She is a Chief of her tribe, the Sack River, where she lives today in Oklahoma. It's a rather large tribe.

To learn more, look up the Chickamauga Cherokee Nation. It's a fascinating study and, for sure, a sad chapter in our history. However, the tribe survives and thrives today due to the ancestors like Stephanie.

Stephanie's horse that she took to Sem was named Soldier Blue. He was a Canadian Thoroughbred.

Today, Stephanie lives on her ranch called the Buzzard Roost Ranch in Pawnee, Oklahoma. She writes children's books and she is married to Gene Jeffords and has 3 fine, young sons.

Sem Recollections:

"I was raised in a small Oklahoma town named Stillwater, home of Oklahoma State University. There was little to do there, but in the 50s and 60s, my daddy made a lot of money and so we moved to a huge home in the country and that was when I met girls who rode horses. My father and I went off to buy a horse and that's when I met Soldier Blue, a malnourished TB and discarded fellow who couldn't race fast enough for the race track so he was put out to pasture. I fell in love with him at first sight and $800 later, we brought my new love back home. Of course, later on he went to Sem with me and it was then I immersed my whole being into so many other athletic programs as well as riding, but riding won out in the end. I loved it. Sem allowed me to be me and for the first time in my life, I was doing what I wanted to do and not some preconceived notion of what my parents wanted me to do. I was finally where I wanted to be and, in life, sometimes we have to search for our star and when we find it, it turns out we are exactly where we are supposed to be."

Adelaide Canipelli '73

Adelaide was in the hunter/jumper class and her instructor was Bernie Gaiser. Her favorite horse was RT. She rode a smaller horse named Cindy (barn name) and her show name was Miss Fortune, a TB.

Sem Recollections:

"I loved Sem – it was the best time of my life. Bernie Gaiser was such a good instructor and friend. He made me a much better rider than I thought possible."

"My best friend was Patti Carroll and we would stay up all night laughing and carrying on."

Life After Sem:

After Sem, Adelaide went to North Carolina and managed a farm in Pinehurst. Then she went to Jacksonville, Florida and taught 42 students to ride under Ray Francis. She traveled the East Coast Shows where she rode and groomed. She went to the Kentucky Derby in 2012 and directed a "HORSE TV CHANNEL" that told all the daily races and handicaps of the each horse.

Adelaide found time to become an X-Ray tech. Today, she lives in Steamboat, Colorado where she enjoys the ski season and living out in the fresh air of the Rocky Mountains.

Janet Sturgill Senft '73

She was in the Equitation Club and rode Carlton's Maybe. Janet says her name was true to her personality: "I never knew if maybe she would jump or maybe she wouldn't."

Janet won 1st place out of 86 riders against Sweet Briar in hunter over fences. She won "Most

Janet Sturgill Senft '73
Image from the Seminary yearbook

Janet Sturgill Senft '73
with Carlton's Maybe or Julie's Easter Boy?
Image from the Seminary yearbook

Improved Rider Award" at graduation in '73.

Today, she lives in Silver Spring, Maryland, but no longer rides, unfortunately.

Janet's recollection is so touching and one riders should pause and reflect on. She captures precisely how the Sem equestrians felt and still feel about those horses: "I was in the equitation program and was lucky enough to have my friend's thoroughbred Julie's Easter Boy or Easter to me. He was there for his education too.

"One evening, when I was homesick, I went to the barn to visit Easter and to enjoy the noises that the horses make in their stalls when they are alone. I found Easter laying down in his stall resting. Usually when you open the stall door, a horse will get up, but if they really trust you, they will usually stay down. Easter and I had a good and trusting relationship so he continued to lay there. I sat down beside his head and he put his head on my lap. We sat there like that together for quite some time and I really enjoyed the warmth of his head on my lap, the sound of his breathing and the sounds of the other horses around us. I have never had another experience like that since then that made me feel so connected to an animal and so calm and relaxed. It still makes me feel emotional whenever I think about that experience."

Lili Elizabeth Rice Kellogg '73

"According to my mother, as a toddler, the second word out of my mouth was horse. Whether or not it was an accurate accounting of my verbalization, I'm pretty sure I was born horse crazy.

"From that standpoint, my career path was determined from the get-go. I was one of the lucky ones. I knew what I wanted to do professionally from a young age and, of course, that was working with horses. As it turned out, my

Lili Kellogg '73
Image from the Seminary yearbook

vision was spot-on and from the day I graduated from college to this day my career path has centered around horses.

"The reason I am telling you all this is because the two years at Southern Sem were instrumental in helping me achieve my career goals. For those of us who are horse lovers, being at Sem was like being in horse-heaven. A group of like-minded young women who were fun and supportive who became lifelong friends. We were a herd of individual equines who had instructors who taught us more than we possibly knew at the time.

"The Department Director, Bernie Gaiser, and the wonderful Katharine Sanford were two of the best at Sem. They used the traditional southern Virginian culture and traditions of that time to serve as a formula of teaching

Lili Kellogg '73 - Voted Best Athlete
Image from the Seminary yearbook

us and giving us an experience like no other school.

"There are so many stories and reflections to recall, so I'll just include a few:

"Miss Sandford was my instructor and the main horse that I rode was Playboy. I LOVED him but, I did ride others too. My first experience fox hunting was at Sem at the Rockbridge Hunt riding (I think) Playboy. It was the cat's meow and I could see how it was even more addicting than horse showing.

"I gained the typical freshman 10 (or is it 20?) pounds plus classmate Pam Price and I were riding our bicycles up the Blue Ridge Parkway. Mr. Gaiser warned us: 'Your calves will get too big for your boots!' Sure enough, one morning after riding class, I couldn't get my boots off. (This was the pre-zipper era.) Someone ran and got Miss Sanford and she cut them off ... right down the back seam.

"At the Sem horse show, during a flat class, we were asked to switch horses to the horse on the left of us and drop our stirrups. I was THRILLED because Butterfly was on my left and Butterfly was a very smooth horse ... at least at the canter. I ended up winning the class because of Butterfly!

"Then there was the time I overslept. If you were late to class it was a cardinal sin! So, I jumped out of bed, whipped on my jeans and flannel shirt, not bothering with underwear, grabbed my chaps and ran to class, making it just in the nick of time. Our class that day was in the lower arena and I was on a young black thoroughbred ... I think it was a mare named Maybe. At the end of class, we were walking back up the hill to the barn, riding on the buckle, when a rabbit jumped out of the bushes in front of my mare. Maybe spun and went bucking down the hill, sending me flying. My arms broke my fall, to a certain extent, but my chest and face hit the ground as well. Nevermind that my front teeth had gone into my lower lip ... more importantly, because the buttons were ripped off my shirt, my main concern was 'I can't let miss Sandford see that I'm not wearing a bra!' as I grasped my shirt together. There probably was some exposure, but not a word was said and my lip healed, although I still have the scars on the inside of my lip to this day.

"As our class was thinking ahead about our educational paths following the two years at Sem, Mr. Gaiser recommended Colorado State University as the leading Equine program in the country. Exclusively because of his guidance, CSU was where I transferred to after Sem. It opened up another world that solidified my career in the equine industry.

"There are many stories to tell about the

parties, being elected as sophomore class president, serving on the May court, and all the fun we had as we bonded over life experiences. A handful of my friends at Sem are still dear friends today even though we live in opposite ends of the country. Sadly, some have passed."

Life After Sem:

Today, Lili is ending a 27-year profession as CEO of The Saddle Equest and is "riding" into a new adventure with STAR, My Sweet Charity.

While at Equest, Lili was a part of the growing program earning great respect in the therapeutic service. One of the big highlights while there was a visit by the Princess Anne.

It was also at that time that Lili received the prestigious PATH International James Brady Award for Professional Achievement given to a person who has made a significant contribution to the industry of equine-assisted services.

Over those 27 years, Lili gave much to the organization and finally decided it was time to retire. She did by returning to North Texas and settling on the Second Time Around Ranch or STAR. She lives there with her husband, Bernie, on a 72-acre ranch along with 40 cows and calves, two hay fields, three horses, 40,000 bees and family dogs and cats.

Joanne (Jo Jo) Greenbaum Schaudies '74

She said, "My horse at Sem was Jim Dandy who was a two-year-old that stayed at Anne Mish's house and later sold to Cindy Cleaves who finally took him to Massachusetts. My instructors were Bernie Gaiser and Katherine Sanford.

"I married a VMI guy in '75. I started show training and became a licensed judge. Thanks to Russ Walther who helped me get my licensing card. I judged the hunter/jumper class.

"I loved to fox hunt, which came from my

Joanne Greenbaum Schaudies '74
Image from the Seminary yearbook

days at Sem in the Rockbridge Hunt.

I judged and showed all over the country and then bought a farm called Surmont in Poolesville, Maryland.

I still fox hunt and now I teach young adults, as well. I own four horses plus a TB named Slow. Today, I raise bassett hounds and show them. I passed on my competitiveness to my hounds. I love them!"

Recollections:

"We all had a special connection at Sem that has lasted a lifetime. Today, my pictures from long ago are my dearest memories."

Vicki Vietsch '74

Her "Heart Horse" was Blue. Bernie Gaiser was her instructor along with Katharine Sanford.

She rode in the Rockbridge Hunt Club and attended Waterstock Training Center in

Vicki Vietsch Schuman '74
Image courtesy of Vicki Vietsch Schuman

Ruth Montgomery '74 with her horse, "Kahlua" and Katharine Sanford at ring at the bottom of the hill in front of Main. Sanford is presenting Ruth with the Most Improved Rider Award.
Image from a contributor

England. She exercised polo ponies and served at Camp Pendleton in the US Navy and as a surgical tech. Then Vicki taught healthcare management at Illinois University. She spent most of her life in Education

Recollections:

"I loved Sem and grew up there. I was extremely shy and my mother passed while I was there and I found the girls so comforting and helpful. It had so much camaraderie. A very good school for me. I chose it for the horse program and loved that, but got so much more than I could imagine from Sem."

Ruth Montgomery '74

She wrote, "Though I graduated in '74, I also went in '75 for some of the animal science classes. My one picture is with my horse, Kahlua and I am with Miss Sanford. It was taken at the ring at the bottom of the hill in front of Main. She is presenting me the Most Improved Rider Award for 1974, which is still on my knick-knack shelf this day. A night or two before this horse show, there was a school meeting for everyone in Chandler. One of the things they announced was that I was getting this award. I didn't hear them say my name and those around me, kept saying, "That's you!" I wasn't listening very carefully and missed hearing I was getting the award. I'm not going to lie, I had an alcoholic or two drinks before going.

"Bernie Gaiser kind of took me under his wing at Sem. I had challenges. I was short and overweight — still am. I also didn't just ride my own horse while there. He had me ride others, including some of the younger less trained ones. He told me I knew how to use my weight to my advantage when riding. You know what? He was right and it all worked out for me.

Cindy Cleaves '74

Cindy's favorite horse was Carlton's Maybe and her Sem horse was Sir Thomas, a rather rough fella to ride. Her instructor was Bernie Gaiser.

Recollections:

"My good friend, Mary Bromm, rode Maybe- a small Thoroughbred, black with his ears pinned back. He was one of those horses with a personality that said, 'Leave me alone. I know what I'm doing.'"

Deb Hogue Hayes '74

Deb said, "I adored Sem from day one. The bonds we all had, and still do. It was an amazing time in my life. I loved horses and had my own named Connemara. I rode the school horse, Kelly, as that was her stable name.

"I rode at the Rockbridge Fox Hunt and loved it. I also did shows with Mary Bromm and Melissa Frank Kaim. We adored Sem and loved the shows.

"We weren't perfect by any means and our greatest adventure was the day we spread soap powder all the way down the floor on our third-floor rooms. We then poured water over it and suddenly we had the biggest slip 'n slide ever. Yes, they caught us, but I don't remember any really bad punishment except we had to clean that hellish mess all up. That floor sure smelled good for quite a while.

"After graduation, I went to State farms and gave lessons. My dear friend, Sabrina Thompson, and I got an apartment together, which was such fun.

"I married and had my children. Today, I have a small low-level hunter/jumper horse farm in rural North Carolina outside Charlotte where I teach lessons and do some eventing as well as boarding. I have eight horses of my own and use them to teach her students. My daughter is a horse trainer and loves horses too.

Mary Bromm '74

Mary enjoyed her years at Sem, but said she was sad that she couldn't bring her own horse to the school. However, she loved Fox hunting and rode the school horse, Banner, who was a dream to go out on. Everyone adored Banner and she was lucky to have that horse to go out

Deb Hogue Hayes '74 with Connamara
Image from the Seminary yearbook

Mary Bromm '74 at Saratoga
Image courtesy of Mary Bromm

Mary Bromm '74 at Rockbridge Hunt
Image courtesy of Mary Bromm

on. Her school horse was Falla, a difficult horse to ride, but she learned how to handle the horse for her classes. Bernie Gaiser and Miss Sanford were her instructors and she truly enjoyed having them.

Fox hunting at the Rockbridge Hunt was her favorite time.

Recollections:

"Sometimes, the VMI guys joined us and much to all our surprise, they wore their uniforms!" she recalled.

"My dear friends were "Spunky" Mullen, Deb Hogue, and Melissa Frank. Super cool ladies who are still my dear friends today.

"I just wish I could have had my own horse there, but, on balance, it all worked out just fine."

Mary lives in Florida but in the summer you can find her at the Belmont and Saratoga with the racing horses she loves and has had 10 years experience with.

Muriel "Spunky" Mullen Andrews '74

Author's Comment: Spunky was just as her nickname suggests - spunky and full of life, AND she remembers everything. It has been reported that "Spunky" was the life of the party while at Sem. A joy to all who know her, I am sure.

Her instructors were Bernie Gaiser, Patty Carroll, and Katharine Sanford Connor. Her horse's name was Duffy, an American Appendix horse which is half-Quarter horse and half-Thoroughbred.

Spunky rode in IHSA competitions. Spunky loved Sem so much she stayed for a third year to get her Animal Science / Equine Studies certificate, which was what several of the riders did down through the years. It was a very important certificate to have as riders went out in the world to teach and train in the horse world.

Muriel "Spunky" Mullen Andrews '74 with Duffy
Image courtesy of Muriel "Spunky" Mullen

Muriel "Spunky" Mullen Andrews '74 with Duffy
Image courtesy of Muriel "Spunky" Mullen

Recollections:

She remembered sneaking the guys into Robey and Zollman's parties out in the county. "We were naughty, but never bad."

"I find this old Chinese Proverb to be the truest way to describe my feelings about my time at Sem. 'There is an invisible thread that connects those who are destined to meet. Regardless of time, place, or circumstance. The thread may tangle and stretch, but it will never break.' The friendships we made are still with us. The school is gone but our sisterhood is forever."

Today, Spunky lives a quiet and lovely life out on Long Island with her horses, a wonderful husband, and all the memories she has stored in her mind and heart.

"Our friendships from Sem were solid and I still enjoy keeping in touch with all my dear friends from Sem. Sadly, there will never be another place like that big, red school on the hill, but aren't we glad we were lucky enough to have gone there?"

Melissa Frank Kaim '74

Melissa recalled that her parents were riding through Virginia and came into Buena Vista and saw the college on the big hill and that was that. They wanted their daughter to go there, so she did.

Her instructor was Katharine Sanford who would make the girls do the 25-minute death trot without stirrups every morning on their horses. It was hell, she reported.

The main instructor and director at the time was Bernie Gaiser, a really good trainer. She did show competitions and fox hunting at the Rockbridge Hunt.

She remembered all the peanut shells on the floor of the stalls. The horses loved to eat them, but weren't so keen on cleaning them up. Her favorite horses were RT and Playboy. She also rode Hickory to the hunt.

Her badge of honor was that she never fell off a horse. Never!

While Miss Sanford was her main instructor, Bernie took all the girls to the shows. She loved Katherine Sanford and said she was such a good instructor along with Bernie Gaiser.

She rode RT to the Christmas parade that year.

Melissa Frank Kaim '74
on Pabst for graduation show
Image courtesy of JoJo Greenbaum Schaudies

Melissa Frank Kaim '74 with Riding Flame
Image courtesy of JoJo Greenbaum Schaudies

Katie Wolf '75 on Dum Dum at the
Lower Ring at the graduation show
Image courtesy of Katie Wolf

After Sem, Melissa went to the University of Miami but didn't like it much. It just couldn't compare to Sem.

She made up her mind she wanted to continue on in education, just not at University of Miami so she applied to Yale, and she got accepted. She said it told the story of how good Sem was that she could go to Yale.

She was and remains to this day a close friend with Mary Bromm. Now retired, Melissa now lives in Lynchburg, Virginia.

Katie Wolf '75

She was an Equitation & Animal Science Major and her instructors were Bernie Gaiser, Katharine Sanford, and Scott Harris.

Patricia Gibson '76

She was an Equitation & Animal Science Major and her instructors were Bernie Gaiser, Katharine Sanford, and Scott Harris.

Her Sem horses were Benchmark and a horse whose barn name was Meal Ticket, but rode as Chat. He would give a few frosty bucks and then break into a brisk gallop.

Barbara Ford '78

After Barbara's (nickname Barbie) graduation from Southern Seminary, she went on to Old Dominion and graduated from there in 1980 with a BA in History.

In the early 70s through the 80s, Barbie was a Judging leader. Then in the 1980s, she became a Therapeutic Riding instructor for 4-H (PERT).

She served as legal secretary for both civilian and US Navy (Norfolk) employers for thirteen years, working in domestic laws and handling adoptions.

In 1986, she graduated from Cheff Center for the handicapped in August, Michigan.

From 1989 to present day, she is owner of Forward Motion Farm, LLC - a blended equine community in Virginia Beach, Virginia.

In 1995, she was certified in PATH, Intl. as a Requested Instructor.

Barbara Ford '78
Image courtesy of Barbara Ford

In 1989, she was Founder and Executive Director of the Equi-Kids Therapeutic Riding Program in Virginia Beach, Virginia.

In 2005, she was the recipient of the James Brady Professional Achievement Awars, PATH Intl. and the recipient of the Friend of Agriculture Award for the City of Virginia Beach, Virginia.

In 2006, she obtained her Certificate of Non-Program Management Tidewater Community College / Norfolk Foundation Workforce Development.

In 2009, she won the National Volunteer Leadership Award - PATH, Intl.

In 2010, she won the Community Legends Award for the Northern Virginia Therapeutic Riding Program Community in Virginia Beach.

She is a current Board member for the Therapeutic Riding Assoc. Of Va. (TRAV) and a present member of Path, INTL., TRAV, AHA, and Animal Response Team of Chesapeake.

Barbara is the mother of twins, Alexandra and Ashley. Ashley is a PATH certified instructor.

Kelli Scarrow Patterson '79

Kelli first learned about Sem in 1977 while working at a horse show as a professional horse show groomer for the clients of George Morris.

After her first year at Sem, Kelli groomed for Olympic rider Melanie Smith.

Her instructor that year was Carl Bessette and her instructor her second year was Pam Doe.

After graduation, Kelli became a rider/trainer and taught in Great Falls, Virginia. She went on to get her BA at George Mason University in Government and Politics.

After GMU, Kelli worked as a legal administrator for a large law firm in DC and stayed for 35 years. Throughout her career, Kelli continued to ride and compete in the Adult Amateur Hunter's shows in Virginia and Maryland on her horses, Sunspot and Donatella.

Kelli is now retired and living with her artist husband, Keith Patterson, on a small farm in

Kelli Scarrow Patterson '79
Image from the Seminary yearbook

Virginia along with horse, Lulu, two mini donkeys, two dogs, and two cats.

Recollections:

"I have many fond memories of my time at Sem, especially the wonderful friends I made there. I loved living in Main, all the horse activities, excursions to Lexington, and sliding down the big hill on trays from the dining hall."

Pamela Stallings Hiner '79

She said, "I rode from the time I was three-years-old. My grandfather, George McConnell, was a big part of the North Carolina State Fair, so I was used to being around horses and other animals. I rode for years after that but not for show, just for fun. When I arrived at Sem, I rode for just one year, but found other interests that made it impossible to keep on riding. They took me away from riding.

"Sem was such a part of my growing up. I loved it. Being so totally overprotected at home, Sem gave me my first taste of freedom and I found myself enjoying so many things I hadn't been able to before."

She went to University of North Carolina State University after Sem and married in '89. Pam traveled around the southeastern states working for Fluor-Construction Company out of Greenville, North Carolina. She said, "It was a happy time and I took a job working for Jimmy Evans, the DA of Montgomery County, Alabama. Then I moved to St. Mary's, Georgia and worked at the submarine base there. Then I divorced and moved back to Wilmington, North Carolina to take care of my mother which ended up lasting for years. I worked in guest services at Kure Beach until my mother fell in 2018. I remained with her until her passing in 2020."

---

* *Carolyn's father was the Buena Vista doctor.*

*Pamela Stallings Hiner '79
in her first year riding photo
Image from the Seminary yearbook*

Today, Pam lives in Calabash, North Carolina across from the Calabash River. She loves it there.

Carolyn Hedrick Williams '79

She said, "I couldn't WAIT to go to Sem because of the wonderful equine program. Even though the school was across the street from my house*, I still lived the normal college life by going to W&L frat parties and meeting my VMI friends. I hung out late in the dorms visiting and studying because all I had to do was literally walk across the street to find my own bed. I also spent my entire day either in classes or at the barn. The one real plus was I had my dog, Sam, with me 24/7. He went everywhere with me because he considered himself my shadow. Although I didn't need a therapy dog, Sam served that purpose to us all at Sem and especially the girls who missed being away from home and missed their pets. He certainly filled

Carolyn Hedrick Williams '79 and her beloved dog, Sam
Image from a contributor

Carolyn Hedrick Williams '79 and her daughter, Carly at the Ocala Reunion in 2023
Image from a contributor

the void for many at school. I lived on Sem Hill so I always felt that the campus was my home and had been since I was a little girl. That place is so special to me in so many ways."

Author's Note: Gee, doesn't Carolyn express how we all feel and still do to this day?

Carolyn had an impact on the school. She continued on after Sem to have an incredible time with several careers.

After Sem, Carolyn opened and still owns a women's clothing store called Hedrick's Clothing for Women in downtown Buena Vista.

She married the love of her life, John Williams, a now retired dairy farmer and they were blessed to have three children: Carly, Cole, and Catie who continue to make them proud as adults.

Carolyn worked as an quine Feed Sales Representative for the Rockbridge Farmer's Cooperation and then went corporate with Southern States as a regional equine feed sales representative for both Southern States and Triple Crown Feed overseeing 43 stores in Virginia.

She stated, "I was Head Coach of the W&L Varsity IHSA Equestrian Riding Team." She was an instructor at Stonebridge Stables in Natural Bridge, Virginia.

She was also the head coach for the Roanoke College IHSA Equestrian Riding Team and ran and operated their own Cherry Hill Farm boarding, training lessons and sales business.

Whew! That's a full lifetime of horses and horse-associated companies.

Today, Carolyn is enjoying her life on her farm in Lexington with her husband and now she is having quite a wonderful time being a GRANDMA!

Suzy Armacost '79

"Wow! Such a great place to grow and spread your wings! Girls from every walk of life, and teachers that made such a difference. Our Animal Science instructor, Betsy Barnes, was

Suzy Armacost '79
Image from the Seminary yearbook

amazing, such a nice major to combine with Equitation. She was so knowledgeable, and that first year raising calves, I felt so at home. I wish she had been there for our next year; it was a little hard getting through Anatomy and Physiology without her. She was getting her Masters in Blacksburg.

"We had a horse judging team and we went to Harrisburg Pennsylvania during the Farm Show for that.

"We went to West Point for the football game between West Point and VMI. We went to parties at The Lodge, Twin Falls, and Phi Si. Raided VMI in the middle of the night, armed with water balloons, shaving cream, and fire extinguishers, after climbing through the men's bathroom, which was referred to as 'The Sinks.'

"Miss Sanford was amazing with her dry sense of humor. She was our Stable Management teacher, riding instructor, barn manager, and confidante. She took us fox hunting and horse showing, and she even took our horses to Charlottesville if they needed to see the vet. I actually taught Stable Management for ten years at Catonsville Community College using her notes from class! I had Baltimore City Mounted Policeman, Baltimore Zoo keepers, and many local people that I taught there. Several I have seen since and still remember me. I had a couple young people that took the class numerous times!"

Terri Wherley '79

Her instructors were Carl Bessette, Director, along with Katharine Sanford, Leslie Brown, Pam Doe, and David Damewood. Her favorite horse was Carlton's Maybe. She recalls the fox hunts at Rockbridge Hunt.

Terri was also assigned to take care of Maybe during her freshman year.

She has a stable in Glen Rock in Central Pennsylvania that specializes in Hunters /

Terri Wherley '79 won the championship at the Blue Rock Show for Large Pony Hunting Division
Image from the Seminary yearbook

Jumpers and Equitation. Some of her riders have competed in IHSA at W&L, Lynchburg, Penn State, Findlay, and a few others.

She enjoys teaching her students today at her farm named Hunter Glen Farm.

Recollection:

"My time at Southern Sem was pivotal in helping me with my business."

More Memories

Seminary Stables in 1974
Image from the Melissa Kaim

Donkey Baseball
Kristie Rind on First Base
Image from the Seminary yearbook

1976 Graduation Horse Show
Image from the Seminary yearbook

Girls and Horses, Please Step Forward: 1980s

The 1980s were set to become the decade of recognition and astounding equestrian achievements for Southern Seminary. All the instructors and efforts put into the equestrian program would now explode in a decade of fame and honor. The Southern Seminary riders had done amazing things before but now they were poised to excel beyond their wildest imagination and take center stage nationally which was unheard of for such a small school.

However, before we move right in to all that, let's take a look back and see where we were as a country in the 1980s.

In 1981, James Earl Carter was defeated by a Californian named Ronald Reagan, a movie star who had also served as Governor. He had personality and qualities that were so outstanding that the people overwhelmingly voted him in knowing that "the Gipper" (as he was known from his college football prowess) would take the country out of the malaise it was suffering with Carter. Uncertainty was all around, but people felt a good measure of hope as well. This would be a time of conservative thought and free market economics which would bring such a boom to America and the country would see more prosperity and advancement than ever before.

Michael Jackson, the youngest son of the "Jackson Five" family would step out of his family and grew to superstar status after his *Thriller* album. He would be the first entertainer

to teach us the "moon walk" and give us music videos the like we had never seen. *Thriller* was an overwhelming and a first-of-its-kind video hit and the young folks took to Michael's songs immediately. He would reign for years as other pop singers came and went. A woman named Madonna sang songs with lyrics we could never have imagined. Whitney Houston, Duran, Duran, Prince, and Cyndi Lauper all joined in to change the world from "Rock and Roll" to techno, jazz, contemporary, gospel and hard rock. Metallica, Bon Jovi, Def Leopard, Queen Kiss, and so many others screamed out and we danced ourselves silly.

TV production was improving and cable optics were a brand new way for TV viewers to enjoy programs like they had not done before. Cable TV would come crashing in and change our availability to get all sorts of new shows we wanted but weren't available to us before. HBO and Showtime became our new friends. MTV became the go-to for young adults. Our culture was changing rapidly. Some said for the better and some said for the worse. We wouldn't really know until much later on. But, for now at least, it was pretty much a time with many carefree days. There were some clouds on the horizon, but we were all too busy with our day-to-day lives to notice. College was the primary goal for the youth and the essential stepping stone to a good job. The job market was a good one and colleges were prospering because so many youths realized they needed to have a higher education to be upwardly mobile in this time of prosperity. For the most part, the nation was settled. No wars were lurking in dark corners and many Americans were becoming very interested in volunteer activities for the underserved.

The Cold War went on but as Reagan continued to pursue peace, we would finally see a warm up of nations and relationships that would bring a new world order to us all.

Tragedy struck the USSR when the Chernobyl hydro power plant melted down and turned into a mega disaster for millions of people.

Then, terrorist attacks began to plague many countries around the world and in some regions, they would spiral out of control for many decades to come. The end of the eighties - November 9, 1989 to be exact - after much political pressure and mass protests, the Berlin Wall was torn down and Germany was again re-united. Great celebrations broke out all over the planet.

Mount St. Helens Volcano erupted in the state of Washington and ash spewed for hundreds of miles, causing hurricane storms and much destruction. Nature's fury was in full force mode and most watched the pictures of that on their television sets, in disbelief.

Movies like *Back to the Future* swept the box office and a game named "Pac Man" kept us all at the arcades. There were many others we loved as well - "Donkey Kong," "Frogger" and "Super Mario" were household names played on the new game system, Nintendo. Perfected from Atari, people now could play more games and spend more time doing so.

Cassette tape decks were all the rage and small cassette tapes could record favorite music for our entertainment. Casual life was changing rapidly and so was the way we used our leisure time.

There was a very dark period to the '80s as well. Assassinations plagued the world when Indira Ghandi, Prime Minister of India, was assassinated as was Anwar Sadat, President of Egypt and a man of peace. President Reagan was shot, but recovered from the shooting.

Yes, the 80s were a time of great change and progress for America and it seemed likewise at Southern Seminary. The increase in riders going to Sem in the sixties and seventies was now becoming a boon for the Equitation program of the eighties. Mr. Robey's far-sightedness with the equitation program was now moving at light speed. He was getting more horses donated to the school while the students applying to go and who were riders was way up in numbers. The program was paying off big time.

Many of the girls were bringing their own horses and the barn that once was adequate was now fast becoming obsolete. The equitation program was well-known and the advertising efforts were in full force, giving many riders all over the country a new college to look at.

An interesting thing to note is that when anything begins to take shape after much hard work and planning, it takes on its own force. That force draws people to it and then things really begin to happen that only a few could imagine.

By the eighties, Sem had earned its solid reputation as an outstanding equestrian arts program and college. This was, what I would say, the pinnacle decade for that program that had been building for years before. The trophy cases were overflowing with the glory the girls would bring back with each competition they entered. The girls weren't any different than others that had been there years before, but the program took on new challenges that brought them to a place they couldn't believe. It was the Directors and Trainers who really made this all happen and it was as if it was all waiting for them to arrive together, as one entity. After the right teachers were there, the program expanded greatly and became the place to be if you were a writer and interested in an equitation major.

Hunter/jumpers, hunt club challenges, dressage riders and shows were the hallmark of Southern Seminary. And none of this would have happened without an outstanding staff, constantly making the riders go beyond what they thought they could. It was a man named Russ Walther who really dug his boots into the program and got it to where it belonged and deserved. Russ was a force of nature and encouraged, trained, taught with a fierce gentleness not many trainers have.

He put together a team like no other and in his time at Southern Seminary, riders became the outstanding team to beat. For a decade plus, the Sem team rode to championships with regularity.

Russ would become a "legend in his own time" for Eastern Equine competitions. He went to Sem a prepared man for the task. He had a vision and he went after it until he got it.

Around now, Russ Walther, an expert horse trainer, was brought to Sem by Ann Mish to see how he might like to work with the girls there. He was a friend of Ann Mish and she finally convinced him to come on board, a decision I am sure he never regretted. With his expert experience, Sem was about to enter a new age of riding excellence.

Russ was excellent at directing the program and training the students, but he was also good at raising money which was a real plus with helping Sem raise the rest of what they needed to begin to rebuild the barn and indoor ring. He went to Nancy's parents and when they heard what they needed, they didn't hesitate to donate money to build the barn. Hallelujah! Sem now had a good start in their fundraising effort for a new barn.

They began to plan and get the layout. When it was finished, the new barn would be renamed from the original Stanford-Mish Arena to the Horton-Ashway Equestrian Center. What a proud and important day that was for Nancy, now an alum, her family, and all the girls who were there and many who would come in the years ahead. A grand achievement! Thank you to all, particularly Russ Walther for raising that money and giving Sem a new, brilliant barn.

However, that wasn't the end of the Ashway generosity. Nancy's mother also bought a six-horse van for the school. Sem was literally rolling now. What a great time it was. Thank you to all who participated in building that new barn.

Julie Whitlock McKee '80

"The riding program was awesome, and I was able to take advantage of all the clinics, showing and hunting, that were offered. My instructors were Carl Bessette and Katharine Sanford.

"After leaving Sem, I began catch-riding for clients, keeping horses fit, showing and selling

Julie Whitlock McKee '80
Image from the Seminary yearbook

horses. I ran quite a few different barns from small private facilities to as large as a 40-stall boarding and lesson facility.

"I was an equine vet tech for over 15 years, which I loved and learned so much, all of which I am still using today.

"I showed my horse, Leica, in the A/O hunters and jumpers, was year-end champion in the 4'6" jumpers. I switched over to eventing with her and we showed through preliminary, winning all the way through the levels.

"I taught hunter lessons to children at a top hunter barn in Atlanta, as well as groomed horses for shows.

"I started my own farm, in 1998 - Fox View Farm. I breed, sell, buy, train, show, and hunt the horses. I currently have 12 horses: five are three-years-old and younger, two are retired, one shows and hunts, and four strictly hunt. I live on 50 acres and love it. We also have four dogs, eight cats and one rabbit! Quite the menagerie!

Recollection:

"I loved Sem. I met some of the greatest women there, and we are all still good friends."

Lisa Barrett '80

Her instructor was Russ Walther. She rode IHSA and won 1980 IHSA Championship.

Recollection:

"I made many friends at Sem. It was a wonderful two years."

Lisa Barrett '80 IHSA Championship
Image from the Seminary yearbook

Melissa Lunning Moore '80

Melissa started riding at eight-years-old and really took to riding. When asked why she chose to go to Sem, she replied, "I had to get out of Dodge and I looked at five other colleges, but Sem was the one! My first year, I majored in Animal Science and my second year was Business."

She worked with Katharine Sanford and said she was "the smartest horsewoman I ever knew."

She rode in IHSA first year and Russ Walther was her second year instructor. She remembers he called her "Mo." She said, "We had fun times with Russ."

Dean Davis was her advisor and she really liked her. Melissa did other sports while at Sem. She was on the tennis team which she enjoyed.

She rode school horses, Joe who was an Appaloosa cross and Carlton's Maybe.

Recollections:

"I loved my two years there and the fact that I still see and speak with the girls today."

After Sem, Melissa bred horses and showed them as well. She has a 33 acre farm with 10 ½ acres cleared. She retired two mares and lives in Suffolk, Virginia.

Due to a health issue, Melissa no longer rides today.

Robin Schuler '81

Robin hailed from New Hampshire where her parents raced Thoroughbreds, so she was always around horses. Quite naturally, Southern Seminary was going to be her college of choice.

She moved to Keswick, Virginia, with her parents while she was still young and that town is near to Charlottsville, Virginia.

When she finally got to Sem, she quickly made close friends with women who were also riders, Holly Hill Wallace and Erin Dirkin. The three were "inseparable." They did everything together and spent a lot of time in the barn so that qualified them and many other girls, as "Barn Rats."

Her major was Animal Science and her instructors were Russ Walther, Pam Doe, and Katharine Sanford. She was also a member of the Equitation Club.

After Sem:

Robin opened up a riding school for children (2-17) and ran it for 48 years. The kids did shows and hunting. She also ran a riding school for kids who had learning difficulties and challenges. That was part of the Oakland School in Keswick, Virginia.

Today, Robin works with race horses and still fox hunts as a member of the Keswick Hunt Club.

She spends her summers in Saratoga at that grand old track where she works with

Robin Schuler '81
Image from the Seminary yearbook

Thoroughbreds, hot walking them, and assisting in many ways.

Recollection:

"I had two great years at Sem and really learned a lot when it came to the anatomy and workings of a horse. It prepared me for all that I was able to do later on. Sem was an incredible experience and gave me a lifetime to be with horses and make forever friends."

Erin Durkin Mitchell '81

Her instructors were Russ Walther, Pam Doe, Katharine Sanford and Carolyn Hedrick, who had just come back to Sem but this time as staff and not as a student. And, of course, Anne Mish was always around for them.

She rode Intercollegiate first year and was President of Equitation Club. Her major was Interior Design (with Frank White) and she had a minor in Equestrian studies.

The horses she rode at Sem were Chat, RT, Carlton's Maybe, as well as another horse named Dragon, who was brought to Sem by another girl, but she didn't exercise him so Erin was asked to do so. She brought her own horse, Toddy, for her second year.

After Sem:

Erin judged shows, something she still does. She was a professional manager and for 25 years she handled the financial part of high-end shows.

She works at UVA in their Clinical Research Department for transplant surgery. Erin also breeds Rottweilers.

Recollection:

"I grew up in a small New Hampshire town and when I got to Sem, it was an entirely new experience. Although the school was small in comparison to many other school campuses, it was a warm and embracing environment. It

Erin Durkin Mitchell '81 with Robin Schuler training a young horse.
Image from the Seminary yearbook

was great fun to be on my own and learning so much. I loved Southern Seminary."

Erin is married and lives in Charlottsville, Virginia.

Renae Boland Sweeney '82

Renae answered this way and it is the sentiment of so many of us all.

"As a rider, I believe we all truly loved having the opportunity to go to Sem and participate in the Equestrian programs. No matter how difficult or challenging, the first years of college can be, it formed us for our futures.

"Miss Walmsley was the first person my parents and I met at Sem. I swear if she had not been there to greet us upon arrival, they would have put me back in the car and taken me home to Minnesota. Miss Walmsley was such a kind and caring person, so welcoming that we were immediately comfortable with our choice of Southern Seminary for my next step. I double majored in General Studies and Horsemanship for my associate degree.

"I found Sem to be a balance of tradition while empowering women to dare do what they dreamed to do. The equine industry is not

Renae Boland Sweeney '82
Image from the Seminary yearbook

Renae Boland Sweeney '82 on her horse, Queen's Castle with another equestrian
Image courtesy of Renae Boland Sweeney

for the faint of heart, it takes determination and true grit to participate at any level, competition or career ... allowing young women to follow their dreams.

"During my years at Sem, my horses came with me: Cinnamon Swirl, my Adult Amateur hunter, Tasha, a young sale horse and Queens Castle, my Amateur Owner hunter who Russ Walther, the director of the riding program, found for me at Louise Serio's Derbydown Stables. Living my dream of not only going to college but taking your horse to college with you!

"The Sem culture provided the best relationships and friends a woman could ask for, friendships that survive the tests of time. I have so many dear friends that I still see and get together with and some that I do not get to see but hold dear in my heart. I was honored to serve as the President of the Equitation Club and speak at the new barn dedication. And then to receive the Ashway Horsemanship Award upon graduation. So much gratitude.

Sem was a space to be ourselves. We were not the typical friends you would find at a college.

We all had different backgrounds and perspectives on life, but horses brought us together, made us family, and we are all so truly lucky for that! Most students went home during the summers between school, however many Sem students had the opportunity to ride and work with some of the greatest horse professionals of that time due to the connections of the Sem instructors. Carolyn Hedrick-Williams, class of '79, Holly Hill Wallace, class of '82, and I had such a great time during our summer adventures at Derbydown Stables with Louise Serio.

Through Sem schooling shows, Classroom classes, Intercollegiate Horse Show, Clinics with established and well-known professionals, United States Hunter Jumper Association Shows, Hunter Trials, Hunter Paces, and Fox Hunting SEM and the Instructors, teachers, and fellow students provided me with some of my greatest memories. From the Hollins Hunter Trials where Katharine Sanford Connor, Carolyn Hedrick-Williams, Liz Millis King, class of '82, Martha Grace class of 82', Elise Roschen class of 82', and myself competed and rode together in the pair's classes. Then our trip by train from Richmond to New York City to experience the epic Madison Square Garden National Horse Show and International Grand Prix. The five of us Sem students arrived to a double room which in New York at the time meant two single beds, we pushed the beds together and made it work. Such wonderful experiences and why I give a big special thanks to my parents.

"I recently stopped competing in the Adult Amateur Hunters and now enjoy riding for pleasure and watching the young girls who lease my horse, Cupcake (Dessert First), at the rated shows in the Children's division. It was exciting to have Cupcake compete in the International Hunter Derby competitions with my current trainer, Nashea Powell of Coriander Farm, in the irons. I always stayed as an amateur and had a wonderful career, from the computer business, and automotive industry (15 years with Mercedes Benz of North America) to currently serving a non-profit, all that has allowed me to support the riding and showing, while enjoying my husband, Ed, and pug, Birdie, in Ponte Dedre Beach, Florida."

Holly Hill Wallace '82

Holly studied riding under Russ Walther and Katharine Sanford.

During her first year, Russ Walther sold Holly a three-year-old horse named Fudge Pie, a "green" horse and inexperienced so Holly had to spend time training Fudge to get him ready to show. Russ helped her train the horse and Holly said, "That was a great experience to watch the horse's progress."

When trained, Holly donated him to Furman College.

For her second year, she bought a horse

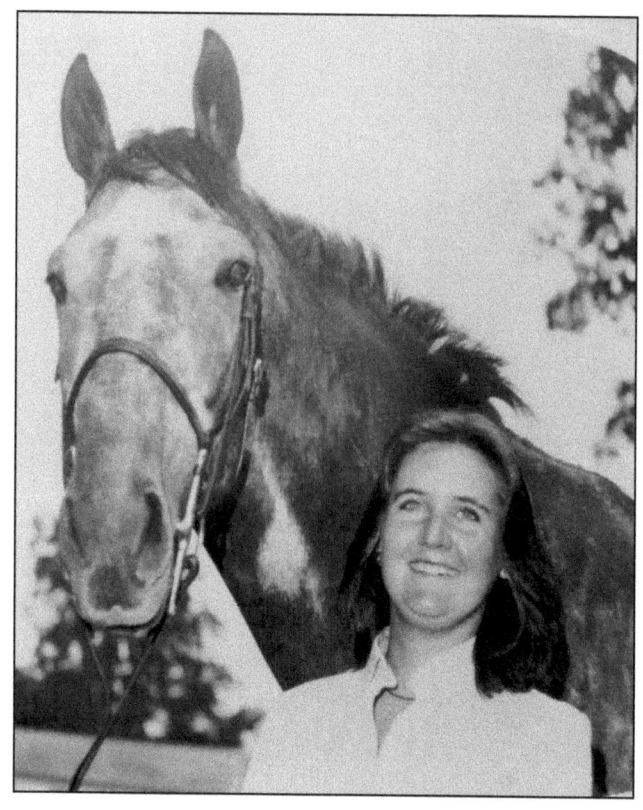

Holly Hill Wallace '82 with Tweed
Image from the Seminary yearbook

Holly Hill Wallace '82
Image from the Seminary yearbook

named Tweed, a very big three-year-old, dapple-gray and bridle trained. Tweed went to shows with Holly.

Holly was on the equestrian team and also Vice-President of the equestrian club in '82. Holly went back for a third year and still rode Tweed and received her Horsemanship Certificate.

Holly chaired a couple of Sem reunions at the magnificent WEC in Ocala, Florida. She brought a lot of memorabilia for us to see and relive old memories. It was attended by many Sem riders and two very important guests: Russ Walther and Bob Cacchione, who told us the history of the Cacchione Cup. It was wonderful to have two men who meant so much to the riding program at Southern Seminary. We all thank you, Holly for the reunions you chaired and the love you have for Sem.

Recollection:

"Out on the road to Hollins and Mary Baldwin, we all had such a good time. I enjoyed the friendships I made at Sem and still see and speak with many of them even today. I wish it could have been a four-year school."

Elizabeth Harvey '82

In Elizabeth's early years, she was riding at 4H level and a few A-level shows in her own state of Washington. Plus, she was doing some three-day eventing.

Elizabeth belonged to the Kin Club. Her mother preceded her and wanted her daughter to go because of the riding team. So, Sem was Elizabeth's first choice. (You can read more about Elizabeth's Mom at the end of this profile.)

Her parents owned a horse named Willie Wonka that Elizabeth rode. The three of them packed up, drove across the country from Seattle

Elizabeth Harvey '81 at the Farmington Hunt
Image from a contributor

Elizabeth Harvey '81
Image from a contributor

to Virginia, and landed at SEM!

As most of the girls, driving up the hill and seeing Main for the first time was a breathtaking experience. She fell in love at first sight. Seattle was a newer city and had no building with that warm and wonderful character.

Russ Walther and Miss Sanford were her instructors.

"After first year, I went back to Seattle and

rode the 'A' circuit from Canada to Oregon training with C&M (Cathy and Mike Crooks) Stables. Their daughter was a hunter/ jumper. It turned out that I saw Russ Walther at the Evergreen Classic Show in Washington that summer. He was judging. It was wonderful to see an old friend, but make no mistake I got no special treatment and I worked hard for the ribbons I won at that show.

"The second year I didn't bring Willie back to Sem and rode RT and Montego Bay mostly. I was Sem's student body Vice President and on the May Court.

"After Sem I went to Washington and was selected for the management training program at the US Bank and then went into the technology world where I've spent my career.

"Unfortunately, I didn't continue down the path of horses as a career and rode only with friends throughout the years. But, not to worry, I became a white water guide for several years.

"I would like to recognize my mother, Daryle Shaffer who went to 'high school' at Sem and graduated in 1954. She wasn't a rider, but a swimmer and swam synchronized swimming while there. She played field hockey with Miss Mish who was still there when I arrived and she was still Director of Phys Ed. My Mom used to say, 'Sem were the best years of her life.'"

Recollections:

"I never understood what my mother was talking about Sem being the best time of her life until I got there and saw the elegance of Main Hall, the beauty of the Blue Ridge Mountains, the quality of the riders, inspiring teachers, and coaches and lifetime friends. Now, I say that Sem were the best time of my life."

Author's Note: I think this sidenote is worthy of telling. Elizabeth wrote, "My Dad went to Princeton and studied under Albert Einstein, the man whose mind was genius. And so is my father's."

Cynthia Tucker Curtis '82

Cynthia went to Sem to ride and ride she did! She is an excellent rider who had been on horses most of her life.

Her instructors were Russ Walther, who was the Director and Katharine Sanford, the Barn Manager.

Cynthia was on the IHSA team and in '82 the team went to Nationals and won! She was a Jumper/Hunter and hunted at the Rockbridge Hunt Club. She took a class from Frank White, and remembers him with fondness. A great guy!

Russ Walther became her dad away from home as he was to many of the girls who went to Sem.

After Sem:

Cynthia continued riding and competing in shows. As I didn't get a recollection from Cynthia, I did get an astounding accomplishment.

At the age of 60, Cynthia began a whole new interest. Riding English all her life, she got on on one of her quarter horses and rode western. Reining was going to be her next conquest. Now this was an entirely wild experience as she was learning to ride, especially at 60, but

Cynthia Tucker Curtis '82 at the IHSA Championship
Image from a contributor

Cynthia was an experienced rider. Still, reining is a whole new kind of riding and teaching for the horse as well as the rider.

In Sem style, this year Cynthia qualified for the AQHA World Championships.

Way to go, Cynthia. You are still making your "sisterhood" proud!

Today, Cynthia lives in Middleburg, Virginia. She continues to promote the town and all it has to offer for riders in America, which is considered to be the Nation's Horse and Hunt Capital.

Well done, Cynthia!

Lori Wright Lehman '83

Lori loved her time at Sem from '81-'83 and said, "I wasn't as talented as some of the girls, but I still supported the team. I did lots of barn duty cleaning up the barn and setting the jumps for shows. The highlight of my time at Sem was setting up for the Nationals competition at Sem in 1983 and we WON!

"Carolyn Williams was my rising instructor as well as my 'Dorm Mom' at Craton Hall."

After Sem:

"I worked at Dr. William Solomon's Pin Oak Farm in Glen Rock, Pennsylvania. It was a large breeding farm of mainly Standardbred horses. I foaled mares, prepped yearlings for sale, and handled Stallions. I did some work with racehorses for a while with James McGreevey and then with galloping horses on a private farm."

After her daughter was born, Lori worked on farms and showed in hunter/jumper at a local show.

She went back to breeding and did everything from general barn work to handling foals, mares, and stallions.

Lori went through a burnout in 2000. All riders go through it at times, working 6 days a week.

Lori Wright Lehman '83 with her horse, The Fox
Image courtesy of Lori Wright Lehman

Lori Wright Lehman '83
Image from the Seminary yearbook

"Then in 2002, I opened my own tack shop called Tackroom Treasures located in East Berlin, Pennsylvania. It is my amazing store today, carrying everything horse and dog and pig.

"I offer English, Western, consignment, and more. Just celebrated 20 years in business. Stop by if you're around these parts.

"Today I have two large ponies and a home-bred Appendix gelding. Still love my barn time and living in the country."

Recollection:

"I remember Beezie Madden, who was a star rider at Sem. We were, and are, so proud of her and her riding talent. I feel very fortunate to have had the Sem experience! I was a true supporter of our team and when we won the 1983 IHSA Nationals at Sem, we were all over the moon."

Renee Birchell '83
Image from the Seminary yearbook

Renee Birchell '83

Her instructor was JT and she always had a horse. She rode with IHSA and was over the moon when they won the Nationals in '83.

She rode dressage on a horse named Nike. His show name was Night Club. After Sem, Renee got married and began a family. A year later, they bought a farm. She had a son, who rode until he was nine and a beautiful girl who rode until she had a bad accident and had traumatic brain injury. But, as she says, "Riders don't much listen to doctors, so her daughter still rides some today."

After a change to her life and a being a single mom, Renee sold the farm and moved down the road so she can still see it every day.

Today, Renee runs her own business, "Equibalance" or "PEMF - Pulsed Electro Magnetic Field." It's a therapy used for horses and syncs their heartbeats.

Renee lives in Barboursville, North Carolina. With children grown and gone, she sold her own horse, and for the first time in 55 years, she no longer owns any horses, but she does manage to work and ride some local horses part-time.

Recollections:

"I was called 'The Chauffeur.' I was the designated driver and the one to drive all my friends back home from the frat parties."

Renee also included a ghost story from Sem. She said that her roommate told her that she woke up one night a saw a little girl sitting on Renee's bed and that she saw people walking around in period clothes. It scared the heck out of them at first, but we got used to it. She swears to this!

Author's Note: I heard other tales of spirits

Renee Birchell '83 at the IHSA Nationals
Image courtesy of Renee Birchell

visiting in Main and there was even a small group of Sem sisters who used the Ouija Board one night and conjured up some very dark spirits. Strange things happened with dogs barking down in the town and visits later in years from these same dark and scary spirits visited all of them.

Katherine McGill '83

She graduated walking on crutches to get her diploma. Her horse fell on the soccer field used for commencement and Katie was banged up badly enough to need the crutches and she couldn't participate in the show. However, she announced for it.

Felicia Guarino Phillips '84

Felicia had an interesting time at Sem. While there, she rode IHSA and went from lowest level to intermediate her third year. Her major was Animal Science and she was also the youngest RA Director. Her instructor was Russ Walther.

Felicia returned to Sem and worked in 1985-1986. She was an active part of the Virginia Horse Center and served as their model when they sent out advertisements to raise funds.

When the Virginia Horse Center opened, Sem had a team of girls who were escorts with the VMI Cadets. The ceremony was held in the VMI Auditorium. "I was one of the escorts," she said.

She was very close to Dean Sherlock and remarked that Paula was a strong woman who believed in protecting girl's rights and integrity.

Recollections:

"Sem was, and is, a strong sisterhood. If you went to Sem, you had a job."

Little known fact about Felicia: she was a pig farmer and raised Mangalitsa pigs. They are the ones that have hair all over them and are said to be the Kobe beef of pork.

Today, Felicia works for FEMA, and is our

Felicia Guarino Phillips '84
Image from the Seminary yearbook

Sem angel who goes in and helps people in disasters.

Julie Olsen Dunson '84

Her instructor was Russ Walther and she was on the IHSA Team. Julie took her two horses to Sem, Catfish Blues and Southern Comfort. She was a member of the Saddle Club.

After Sem:

Today, Julie owns a farm called Sullystone Stables in Monterey, Virginia. It's about an hour and a half northwest of Sem.

She has a 4-H Club that she enjoys and works with the kids learning important skills. Its name is "The Highland Hoofbeats."

Recollections:

"We won the Nationals in '84; our team was incredible. I remember Beezie Patton and I have to say, I idolized her. She was one amazing rider. We all appreciated her talent so much."

Julie Olsen Dunson '84
Image courtesy of Julie Olsen Dunson

A "show of support" sticker for the Sem Riders
Image from one of the contributors

Elizabeth "Beezie" Patton Madden '84
Image from the Seminary yearbook

Elizabeth (Beezie) Patton Madden '84

Beezie's story is one that could take up an entire book, but for this journal, she is a class member and fellow team competitor of Southern Seminary.

Joining the school riders, Beezie came from Milwaukee, Wisconsin and desired to go to a school where equestrian and advanced equestrian studies were given. In Virginia, on that big hill in a small town, she found that place. A somewhat shy and quiet girl, by all accounts, Beezie found Sem a place as so many other girls did, to be a welcoming, nurturing environment where she could spread her wings and fly. And fly she did. When Beezie got on her horse, she looked as a goddess on top of Pegasus, taking on the course at hand and then jumping with the ease and grace of a gazelle.

Beezie competed in IHSA competitions while at Sem, winning with her team. The ribbons and championships that came home in those years were hard-fought and many in number.

Her team mates and friends say she was not only an amazing rider, but she enjoyed other sports such as basketball and softball. She was a true sportswoman as well as an excellent student.

Elizabeth "Beezie" Patton Madden '84 on school horse, Chat
Image from the Seminary yearbook

Elizabeth "Beezie" Patton Madden '84 Olympic Champion and Seminary rider hoists a well-earned trophy in the air
Image courtesy of John Madden Sales

In 1984, Beezie won the prized Cacchione Cup for Intercollegiate excellence. She was Valedictorian of her graduating class of 1984.

In 1985, Beezie launched her "Grand Prix" show jumping career. She went on from Sem to become a US Olympic champion in hunter/jumper.

Aside from the many championships she won, Beezie Madden was the FIRST WOMAN to achieve $1 million dollars in earnings for show jumping.

Yes, we are all proud of you, Beezie, and what you bring to women, and young girls and boys who have dreams of one day being like you and taking to the course and jumping their way into the Olympics.

What a grand equestrian life you have lived, Beezie, and to think, it all started long ago with a group of other young women who would go on to reach their goals and dreams in the Equine world.

Recollection:

"I was lucky enough to have both Russ Walther and JT as instructors when I was at Southern Sem. I also have fond memories of Miss Sanford and Carolyn Hedrick Williams. At the time, I don't think you could have found a better team of people to learn skills of horsemanship and competition. Southern Sem was a small school with a close-knit community feeling where friendships and skills in teamwork were formed. We had lots of shows that were fun and successful, but I think my most memorable was the final at Harrisburg, Pennsylvania Arena Farm."

For more information on Beezie Madden

and her illustrious career, just Google "Beezie Madden." She has had an astounding career in the Equestrian world. We couldn't be prouder of you, Beezie.

Tracy Scott '85

Tracy comes from Simpsonville, Kentucky and she has a farm called Skyland Farm in Kentucky for retirement horses

She rode on the IHSA Team (hunter/jumper) and her instructor was JT. She adored Katharine Sanford and was able to fox hunt with her which she loved. Tracy still fox hunts today.

Her favorite horses were Mystery Man, Benchmark, and Churchill.

She rode lessons with her "bestie" Beezie Patton Madden and they still remain good friends.

Tracy Scott '84 on Night Flight in Texas
Image courtesy of Tracy Scott

Captain Tracy Scott '84 on the left
Image courtesy of Tracy Scott

After Sem, Tracy became a pilot and flew with American Eagle for two years and then decided to fly the big planes for UPS and she's been with them for 31 years. So, today we call her Captain Tracy Scott.

Tracy names her horses after flying terms at UPS. She pays homage to UPS for the career she has been afforded so she can pay to compete. Here's to Night Flight and On Time.

Tracy said, "Sem was all about riding. I grew up there."

Tracy Scott '84 on Pinto Next Day Air at the KHP Show in Kentucky
Image courtesy of Tracy Scott

Jennifer Breeding Tingley '85
Image from the Seminary yearbook

Jennifer Breeding Tingley '85

Jennifer brought her horse, Farrell, a TB, to school. She remembers he wasn't exactly thrilled or fond of his reduced turnout.

Her riding instructor was mostly Sem grad Carolyn Williams and occasionally instructors Pam Doe, Russ Walther, and JT Tallon.

A sad act of fate happened to Jennifer when she busted up her knee in November and couldn't ride again until that was healed. So, she wasn't able to show, but she could help in prep work for the other riders. Go Jennifer!

Jennifer said, "My first impression of Sem .. It was so beautiful and I loved the majestic Main Hall and the view of the mountains. Instantly, I fell in love with the Blue Ridge Mountains and dreamed of returning one day.

"Miracle of miracles, I did in 2017. My VMI husband, Dave Tingely (Class of '85) and I bought a farm and we now call Rockbridge County our home."

Jennifer's class performed a most important task. Folks were looking around to determine where they should build the Virginia Horse Center. They went on three class trips over to Lexington to walk through the determined course which WE DESIGNED! How proud and honored we were to be able to do that. It has been so neat to see how that center has grown and evolved over the years.

"Fun trivia: this is how fate works sometimes. I went to Sem for the horse program and so many of my friends would say, 'Are you going there to get your M.R.S. degree?' I didn't quite understand. They said, 'You know, with two all male schools six miles away?' Honestly, I did not know that because I was so involved with the horses. As stated, I ended up meeting and marrying the love of my life, Dave Tingely, class of 85."

A side note from Jennifer: "I would like to add that one of the senior riding students when I was a freshman was a quiet and lovely Sem sister whose riding (jumping) was like no other and loved to watch her. I kept out of her way being she was an 'upper class mate' and I only a first-year girl. She had a wonderful partnership with the horses she had brought to school. Quite a special rider and it turned out that after Sem she went on to join our American Olympic Equestrian team and become one of the all-time great jumpers in the world today. We all love you and cheer you on, Beezie Madden!"

Diana (Dee Dee) Grzeszczak Calegari '85

Dee Dee thinks she rode Sem horses Chat and Gus. Her instructor was instructor was JT.

Diana "Dee Dee" Grzeszczak Calegari '85
Image from the Seminary yearbook

Diana "Dee Dee" Grzeszczak Calegari '85
Image courtesy of Diana Grzeszczak Calegari

She was on the equestrian team and was on the team that won the Nationals in '84 and '85.

Recollections:

Dee Dee remarked, "Sem was a sisterhood and friends made there lasted a lifetime. It was an amazing place to be the years I went. The riding talent and IHSA nationals were unreal. Proud to be such a part of that riding Sem history."

Dee Dee remembers an endearing moment with Beezie Patton Madden and her parents. They were at a horse show and returning home when our bus broke down and the Pattons gave Beezie and some of us a ride back to school. It was such a lovely gesture from very lovely people."

After Sem:

In the early '90s, Dee Dee volunteered for EQUIKIDS, a riding program for people who were paralyzed. She volunteered to work for a former Sem graduate, Barbara Ford, who owned the business and looked for younger Sem graduates to volunteer for her program which was a growing industry in Virginia Beach.

She married a VMI graduate who made a career out of the service and when the author was meeting up with Dee Dee a few years ago, Dee Dee was with her grown son who had just been accepted into VMI. They were thrilled.

Kathy (Kat) Cullen Henley '85

Kat Cullen was an excellent rider and was on the 1984-1985 IHSA team which won the '84 IHSA Competition held at Sem that year.

Her horse was Carlton's Maybe and her Sem riding story can be seen through the pictures she sent in.

Kat graduated with an AS degree in Equine Management and an AS degree in Liberal Arts.

Today, she lives in Painter, Virginia on

Margaret Katherine Cullen Henley '85
Image from the Seminary yearbook

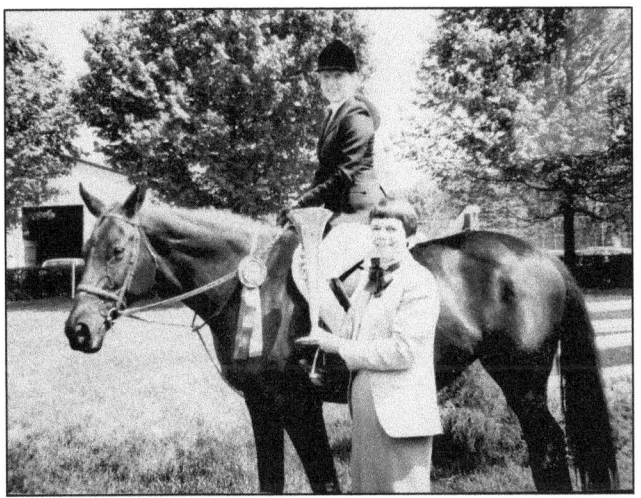

Margaret Katherine Cullen Henley '85 with President Joyce Davis holding the Winner's Cup after winning the IHSA Competition

Image courtesy of Margaret K. Cullen Henley

Virginia's Eastern Shore.

Recollection:

"My years at Sem will always be some of my happiest memories. I chose to attend Southern Sem because it was the number one college in the country for riding and I could not see my life without horses at the center. I loved riding on the team and learning from Katharine, Carolyn, JT, and Russ. They each had wonderful insights to share with us. While I was far from being the top rider, we all lifted each other up with our love of horses. Two of my fondest memories would have to be winning the Southern Sem College Horse Show my freshman year in 1984 riding Carlton's Maybe. She was a great mare! Joyce Davis presented me with the trophy that now includes my name and is still on display at Southern Virginia University. Another proud moment for me was serving as an usher for the Governor of Virginia at the signing for the Virginia Horse Center which is still a major horse show location today and used for much more. While the staff and fellow students remain as my fondest memories, along with W&L, VMI and townies, the horses cannot be left out. A few that pop in my mind are Carlton's Maybe, Mr. Pibb, and Leo. I am truly sorry that Sem does not still exist as it was when I was there. I believe that many young ladies would grow in self-worth and confidence there especially in this crazy world we live in today.

"As an adult, riding did not always fit into my life, with children, and teaching school. My love has always remained strong for Sem and horses. At 58, I recently started riding again and find it so therapeutic. I don't have any desire to return to the show ring, but an afternoon of pleasure riding in a field is heavenly to me now.

Amy Squier Perez '86

"I just loved my time at Sem. I married a VMI boy and I am still married to him."

"My instructor was JT and my favorite horse was Checker Chip, a Chestnut. He was a sweet horse, but he was hard to control in his place."

"I still ride today and am a certified Therapeutic Riding Instructor, working with special needs folks on horseback."

Sylvia Hoffman Cole '87

Sylvia had an unusual experience at Sem. She loved to ride and had been riding since she was a young girl, so choosing Sem was a natural fit for her.

At the end of her freshman year at Sem in 1986, Sylvia was already proving herself as an excellent rider and an all-around good athlete. As fate would have it, she was out riding and took a nasty fall off her horse. That fall would result in many injuries and a few badly broken bones when the horse landed on top of her. The result was she had to withdraw temporarily from school, which meant going home and letting her body heal.

She was determined to return better than ever, and that day finally came for her.

Her instructors were JT, Carolyn Williams, Katharine Sanford, and Chris Wynne, who was replacing Russ Walther who had left earlier after an incredible time making history for Southern Seminary.

She returned in the spring '87 in her second year second semester. She had played softball, as well as riding, in her first year before the accident and upon her return she went back to the softball team as well as proceeding to ride. She was able to get back in shape and began competing once again. The team went to the IHSA Nationals that year where the girls saw Russ Walther, the former Director of the riding program.

JT Tallon was now the Director. She also returned to the riding program and participated at the IHSA Nationals that year. Sem won at the Nationals with Russ and JT looking on, proud as could be.

Author's Note: At this point the Sem team had won Seven Nationals Titles and then returning to the champions ring when they won again in '87 and '88!

Sylvia was proud to be a part of the them.

After Sem:

Sylvia had always been a part of a 4-H Club where she lives in the Blackwater area of Virginia Beach. She quickly began a business and worked with youths and some elderly folks from all around the area.

She strongly recommended kids to the 4-H programs near them and began to teach them in an advanced horse program so they could truly understand the horse. It was imperative for her to make sure they knew all about the anatomy of the horse and her program provided a one-year course project that each young person could take if they wanted. That program taught them to keep organized records of costs for having a horse, taking care of a horse, the costs of having a horse, and so on. The outcome of the project was that kids gained a good deal of respect and discipline in their lives, and after testing, they were knowledgeable about all areas of horsemanship and stable management.

Today Sylvia enjoys teaching and training young people. She is still involved with her lifelong passion for the 4-H programs in the area and is on the All Star 4-H advisory Board.

Sylvia enjoys seeing Barbara Ford (another Sem Equestrian) around that area and she holds a summer camp each year for the kids. She teaches them on TBs, Quarter Horses, Welsh ponies, Warm Bloods, and Hunter/jumpers.

Recollection:

"I loved Sem and I have used the tools from the Equine Management / Vet Science program I majored in. I learned so much there about the horse that I still teach today."

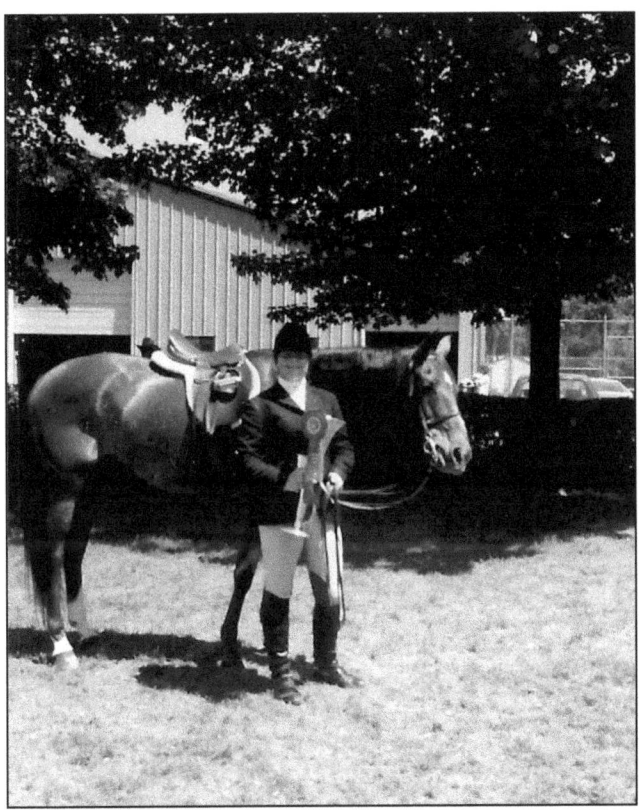

Druanne Paulk Roberts '87 with her horse, Spellbinder, holding the Graduation Cup
Image courtesy of Druanne Paulk Roberts

Druanne Paulk Roberts '87

She in the Kin Club; her sister Missie went to Sem in '92.

Druanne went off to Sem at age 16, very unusual, but then so was Druanne.

She wanted to go there for a very long time and Miss Mish advocated for her and they decided to let her attend.

She stayed and went a third year as well to get her Equitation Certificate. This was the first year that particular certificate was available to the riders.

She rode in the hunter/jumper class and her instructors were Russ Walther, JT, and Katharine Sanford; Carolyn Hedrick Williams also helped train Druanne.

The first year she rode About Time and the second year she brought her horse, Spellbinder.

Her "big sister" was Stacy Robinson Sullivan (class of '84) who was very helpful to Druanne.

She would sometimes help braid the horses and the girl's hair as well before a show.

Druanne was on IHSA team.

One special memory was when the riders that year went to Harrisburg, PA to see Beezie Patton Madden ride in that show.

Druanne boarded her horse, Spellbinder at Leslie Brown's farm because there weren't enough turn out paddocks.

She did enjoy fox hunting at the Rockbridge Hunt once in a while. They had gorgeous terrain there, perfect for fox hunting.

Druanne received the Commencement Day Trophy at graduation, in 1987, which would happen again to her sister, Missie in '87. They would be the only sisters ever to win that award!

After Sem:

Druanne trained in Mississippi for a while. She helped her sister braid for a while and they went into business with Magna Wave, a machine that helps aid horses through shock therapy for many horse injuries rather than surgery.

Druanne has no horses today; her last one was in 2021.

Recollections:

"I loved Sem and when the seasons change to fall, my mind goes back to Sem, so I get out my yearbook and there I find the days I had forgotten.

"I remember seeing an ad for Sem in the *Practical Horseman*. I knew then and there I was going to go to Southern Seminary. The school offered all aspects of the sport of showing horses with the exception of the World Cup and Olympic. Our program was an individual sport: just you and the horse. Sem had the top riding program and trainers so, for me, to be a part of that team, competing in a sport I loved, was my dream. The school allowed me to immerse in the horse industry - it was magical."

Holly Barker Dawson '87
Image courtesy of Holly Barker Dawson

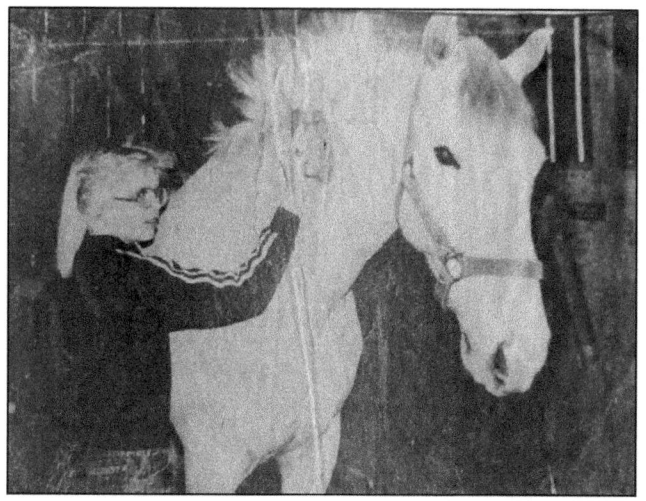

Holly Barker Dawson '87 grooming Warlock in the Sem Barn
Image courtesy of Holly Barker Dawson

Holly Barker Dawson '87

Holly had been riding for years by the time she got to Sem. She did lots of showing and was rated A level.

She majored in Physical Education and Horsemanship with Anne Mish.

Her instructors were mainly Russ Walther and JT. However, Katharine Sanford, Miss Saunders, and Anne Mish taught some lessons with Holly as well.

Holly took her own horse, Warlock, to Sem. He came from Fredericksburg and was 15 when she got him. He was a TB Welsh Cross Gelding.

Holly rode in all the shows at Sem and showed at "The Barracks" in Charlottsville.

Warlock lived to be 27 years old. It was so sad when he died.

After Sem:

Holly became a nurse and practiced for years; today, she is a Licensed Massage Therapist.

She did a lot of trail riding.

Holly enjoys life in the Tidewater area outside of Suffolk, Virginia. She missed her friends from Sem, so much that she started a chat group. Now, she enjoys re-connecting with her Sem Sisters from long ago.

Lisa Berney Aaron '87

Her instructors were JT and Katharine Sanford. She loved animals of all kinds but particularly horses.

She did not compete but rode for Physical Education on RT. Her major was Animal Science and she lived both years in Main.

After Sem

Lisa went to Washington, D.C. and worked for Department of Defense with animal health.

She lives in Harrisburg, Pennsylvania and still rides today although she does not compete.

Recollection:

"Coming from a small town, I wanted to leave and experience new places and new things. I loved Virginia and Southern Sem. I particularly liked the experience of working with horses and being a part of a great small and intimate school."

Lisa Shelton '88

She rode while at Sem and her instructor was JT.

Lisa worked for the government and then retired and became a writer. She runs a turkey farm and lives a good life in a small area between Richmond and Charlottsville, Virginia. She has given us a beautiful memory of our alma mater. She is, indeed, a talented woman, as we all are.

Enjoy the beauty of her words and being a part of such a wonderful place and sorority of women that we all share still today. Thank you, Lisa!

"It's with great fondness that I look back upon my time at Southern Seminary Junior Women's College. The two years passed quickly, but the memory is as clear as yesterday. The sounds of trays rattling, the smell of waffles drifting in the air and Jim (cafeteria head) staring out from behind that auburn mustache at the girls that he was responsible for feeding that morning. No sooner had breakfast begun than

Ribbons belonging to Lisa Shelton '88
Image from a contributor

Lisa Shelton '88 with Bekka,
granddaughter of Olympic Ferro
Image courtesy of Lisa Shelton

it was over, with an occasional break out of a food fight. Then onward to the smell of hay in the barn and the music of horses feeding before the first riding class of the morning.

"Young ladies lined up on the rail to watch JT Tallon give riding lessons, absorbing his training with the smell of crisp mountain air all around us. I recall the feeling of balance and harmony JT taught as he held the lunge line, my irons crossed and arms outstretched, posting till my legs where secure. He was my key contributor to riding success which led to all my ribbons. I was caught with total unawareness on my graduation day in May of 1988 as I was handed the double "S" letters for riding at Sem. Yes, I went on to two other colleges and several other degrees, but none were held so dear as my days as a Maid of the Mountain.

Katie Gaines Van Alstyne '88

She said of Sem, "Best time of my life."

Her instructor was JT for a short while; then it was Chris Wynn and Nancy Peterson

Katie rode on the IHSA team and says she won her class in Indianapolis to contribute to the team victory. Go Katie!

After Sem:

Katie went on to Hollins and then to the National Park Service on Cape Hatteras. Up next was Monmouth Cave, Kentucky, and then to Great Basin in Nevada, and then on to the Grand Canyon in Arizona where she met and married her husband, Todd Van Alstyne.

"We moved to Rapid City, South Dakota, both working for the U.S. Forest Service and we worked there serving the regions of Washington State and Oregon implementing Wildfire Crisis Strategy through bipartisan infrastructure laws.

Katie Gaines Van Alstyne '88
Image courtesy of Katie Gaines Van Alstyne

"I met some amazing girls at Sem and reconnecting with them is such a pleasure. Patty Messina, Lisa Gray, Amy Gates and Sugi Smithson Dewan who was my maid of honor."

Author's Note: It's so wonderful to have friends like we all do for a lifetime. That tells us how wonderful Southern Seminary really was.

Katie said, "I still ride and get more and more comfortable with going fast into the world of 'Eventing' with my OTTB, Beau. His show name is Fun & Games."

Recollection:

"Sem gave us a chance and opened doors! From there, it's up to you and sometimes luck!"

Today, Katie lives under the open skies of Montana.

Katie Gaines Van Alstyne '88
Image from the Seminary yearbook

Tamara (Tammy) Ginaven Robbins '88

Tammy was a member of the Kin Club at Sem. Her mom, Nancy Ginavan, was a '59 graduate and a rider. She also had an aunt and a cousin who went to Sem.

Her favorite professors were Robert Bedell who taught English and John Adams who taught math.

Her instructor was JT and her favorite horse was Playboy.

She remembered, "I looked forward to checking the mail box for care packages. Food at Sem was delicious. At this time, the girls went through a food line and then had to find a table."

Author's Note: Big changes came in the years going forward. We had assigned seats in the dining room and we were served our food mostly by wonderful town women in 1966-1967.

Tammy's roommate was Cathy (Cat) Harris and she recalled study nights at VMI library and movie nights in the dorm.

After Sem:

She transferred to Virginia Tech that was known as VPI years before and then graduated from Mary Baldwin.

Tammy raised and sold ponies with her family and also worked with parents in their embroidery business at horse shows.

Today, she works for State Farm. She married Trent Robbins and moved to Virginia Beach, Virginia.

Recollections:

"Loved Sem. It had a small, family feel."

The eighties proved to be everything that many people envisioned it to be. It managed to take the Southern Seminary riding program to glory and fame all around America, and even beyond our borders

Young women were reading the ads in many magazines and deciding to go to this college. So many dreams were being fulfilled at Southern Seminary and now, with the third-year equitation study to receive that coveted certificate, Sem was the recognized college for riding. It had accomplished all that Margaret and Russell Robey and the many instructors that came through that school, hoped it would become.

Patty Messina Panzarella '88
Image from the Seminary yearbook

Patty Messina Panzarella '88

Patty had been riding for years before she arrived at Sem. In fact, she was a successful Jr. Rider.

Her instructor was JT and she rode two successful years on the IHSA Team. She was a hunter/jumper. The team won the Cartier Cup. Patty won IHSA in '87 and '88.

She loved fox hunting and riding with Katharine Sanford.

Patty took a year off after Sem and then in 1989 realized her dream and began her professional horse business. She trains students and sells horses.

Recollection:

"I actually did not want to go to college. I knew what I wanted to do and I didn't need to go to college to be in the horse business. Well, my parents insisted I go and they said I could bring my young horse with me, so I went. I am beyond grateful for them pushing me because it was the best experience in my life. It was the first time I was part of a team and I absolutely loved it after always riding as an individual. (I was not involved in high school with sports or anything.) Today, I meet up with my Sem Sisters throughout the year when I can, and I love them dearly!"

Christmas Memories

Southern Seminary Christmas Tree in the 1980s
Image from a contributor

Druanne Paulk '87 - Christmas Horses Parade
Image from the Seminary yearbook

Santa and Mrs. Claus on Horses in 1984
(Beezie Patton and Stacy Robinson)
Image from the Seminary Yearbook

The End of an Era: 1990s

The nineties were transformative years in America, and even more so for Southern Seminary. The country would see the emergence of Google and Amazon. Thos two behemoths would change America, and the world, forever. "Google" became a household word that would send us off to our computers and cell phones to discover whole new ways of learning and ordering goods that would be delivered right to our doors in the blink of an eye. Technology was now moving at light speed. We had no idea where this would go, but go it would.

The movies we loved were *Titanic*, which was the first movie to earn a billion dollars. *Toy Story* was a delightful tale with a looney character named "Buzz Lightyear." This was the first specially animated cartoon and we loved it. After years of work by Animated Studios, Disney bought it and it has been known as Pixar ever since.

The Women's World Cup of Soccer (Football) FIFA was established. American women have since won the cup four times.

The world saw the collapse of the U.S.S.R into many countries who returned to their original names. Today they are Armenia, Azerbaijan, and Georgia.

Nelson Mandela went from being a prisoner in South Africa to its first President.

The TV sitcom *Friends* stole our hearts with characters we all could relate to.

In April 1995, there was the Oklahoma City bombing, leaving many people dead and a na-  tion stunned. Our first really bad terrorist act.

Our space shuttle *Atlantis* docked with the Russian station.

A celebrity name Oprah Winfrey burst into our living rooms and held us captive with her programs, advice, and her intrepid book club where books she picked skyrocketed to instant fame and fortune.

TV audiences sat utterly stunned and unbelieving when it was announced that Princess Diana, Princess of Wales, had been killed in an automobile car crash in a tunnel in Paris. It left us all paralyzed at our televisions for days as mounds of flowers were put in front of the gates of Buckingham Palace.

Tiger Woods makes history by shooting 270 over a 70-hole tournament at The Masters in Georgia. He became an instant hero of the golfing world.

Our beloved *Seinfeld* ended its run. We were sad to see him and his cohorts leave us. He was a seriously funny man as were the entire cast.

President Clinton faced an impeachment but not a conviction.

The Columbine high school massacre devastated us and, as we look back now, was a harbinger of other dreadful tragedies in schools.

As we will see, Southern Seminary riders kept on coming to learn and compete in the programs offered in equitation studies as well as business and other areas of study. They continued to win their competitions and ride to the hunt on weekends at the Rockbridge Hunt Club. However, four-year educations were becoming much more available and competing with the two-year schools. And many women were choosing the larger campuses which were also co-ed. For the most part, life was good and America was enjoying unprecedented wealth as never before, and there were opportunities that women could now take advantage of that were out of their reach before.

Sem continued to hold its own; however, in this very competitive atmosphere, dark clouds were gathering on the horizon that no one wanted to see or dared to think of that could possibly affect such a school such as Southern Seminary. It was a tradition ... a way of life for young women and had stood the test of time. Yet some knew that time might be running out for this kind of school, but many ignored the signs. That thought was kept at arm's length and not discussed. To do so might just bring down the 129-year-old ship.

Kimberly Fulton '91

Kim rode school horse, Cowboy, during her first year, but took her horse, Black Magic the second. Cowboy was her horse at that year's Christmas tree parade.

She was the RA for Crayton Hall both years and enjoyed that experience with the girls who roomed there. While at Sem, she made good friends that she still sees today.

Kimberly Fulton '88 with her dad
Image courtesy of Kimberly Fulton

She was a hunter/jumper and was there when they brought fox hunting in to the ring.

Her instructors were JT, Katharine Sanford, Leslie Brown, an older woman named Sarah, and Kim Diehl for the first year. She would work sometimes at JT's farm in Lexington and loved that opportunity.

Kim boarded her horse, Black Magic, during the second year at Leslie Brown's home.

She was an Equine Studies major and achieved an Associates in Equitation certificate.

Kim was not on the IHSA Team but would help them when there was a show at Sem. She was proud to have won the "Ashway Sportsmanship Award."

After Sem:

Kim returned to her home in New Hampshire and began working at a retirement community. She would ride a little but then

On the right is Black Magic, the horse of Kimberly Fulton '88, with Damast on left.
Image courtesy of Kimberly Fulton

gave it up totally and took on dog training in AKC Agility Competitions. Her Border collie and corgi have competed at Westminster Dog Show Agility Trials.

Recollection:

"Sem was the best time of my life, as I look back now. I made lifelong friends. It was a very special place. I had one, very special memory. That was when Ann Krazinski, an Olympic Champion, came to campus and gave a clinic. It was super magical and thrilling to meet her and have her work with us."

Renee Clark '91

Renee rode for three years on the IHSA Team at Sem in the 90s. She rode in the IHSA Nationals with JT.

Sarah Irvine was her instructor as well as JT, who she thought was amazing!

Renee lived in Main for her first year, then on the fourth floor for her second, and the third year house, which no one knows the name, while she studied for the Equine Certificate.

After Sem:

Renee went on in her education to receive

Renee Clark '91 and her horse, Bubbles, at the Syracuse State Fair
Image courtesy of Renee Clark

her teaching degree and also taught Animal Science at a vocational school for 15 years.

Recollections:

Sadly, she put her show horse, Bubbles, down eight years ago. She purchased that horse at Sem so that made it equally difficult.

Renee no longer rides today but she looks back fondly of the times she had at Sem with all her "Sem Sisters" and the times they had together, riding and enjoying themselves. She still keeps in touch with many from her class.

And, she tells of the wonderful and fun trips to IHSA events, but none topped the trip and competitions at Nationals.

Lisa Barnett Booth '91

Her instructor was Sarah Vorhies. Lisa's favorite horse was Jay Midnight Rambler. She wanted to ride him for schooling events and shows, however, she mostly drew Fox who happened to be a good ride.

She was on IHSA Team from end of 1990 and then won Regionals and Zonals in 1991. She was Reserve Champion, Advanced walk/trot and was awarded 3rd place – Advanced walk/trot.

Sadly, Lisa did not go to Nationals, missing by one place.

She said, "I have such fond memories of Sem. The parties at Zollmans and Hops at VMI, the Sem mixers. I lived in the third-year house my second year and enjoyed that. Made many good friends at Sem and still communicate with them on Facebook."

After Sem:

Lisa worked at Saddle Breeding and Hackney Pony Show and breeding farms.

She went on to ride and show in Western Pleasure – Ranch House doing speed events, trail challenges, and team penning. She also gave Western lessons.

Since 2016, Lisa gave up owning horses and started a pet sitting business, so she is still around horses all the time.

Missie Paulk Morrissey '92

She also belonged to the Kin Club. Her sister, Druanne Paulk Roberts, graduated in class of 1987.

Her instructor was JT during her first year and then JT retired and Amy Reistraup and Carolyn Williams came on as instructors for the girls. Later in her second year, Chris Brown joined the instructor team.

She belonged to Equitation Club and rode competitions as Open Rider in highest level of hunter/jumper. She rode in IHSA competitions.

During her second year, she brought her horse Hank (show name Silent Persuasion) to Sem and boarded him at Leslie Brown's farm.

Missie was qualified to go to Nationals as part of the team. She showed in Open Over Fences and was the second highest point rider. She won the Cacchione Cup at Zone 4 finals at Moorehead College in Kentucky 1992. She remembered another great win over Hollins to win another competition. That show was at Duke.

At graduation, President Davis awarded Missie the Graduation Cup that her sister had received in '87, making them the only sisters to win that award. Missie rode her favorite Sem horse, Simon. Fun fact: Missie's roommate Stacey Whitecross won the Graduation Award the following year in '93.

Missie Paulk Morissey '92
Image from the Seminary yearbook

Missie Paulk Morissey '92 winning finals at Nationals
Image courtesy of Missie Paulk Morissey

Missie also shared some of the ghost stories in the house they lived in. Some of them even said they saw spirits in the night. She wasn't the only one who had stories of other spirits roaming the halls and residences of Southern Seminary.

Recollection:

Missie recalled the smell of the barn and how she loved it. She loved walking from Main to the barn for lessons. All the friends she made while at Sem and the "fun friends and fun nights" they had at their third-year house.

She recalls going to shows with JT and how he never stopped, not even for a bathroom stop. No, not ever! The girls used the rare gas stops to "go" and even then, it wasn't in the prettiest of places out back of the gas stations.

Missie went back to Sem for third year and lived in a house across from the barn. All the girls became fast friends and still are today.

After Sem, Missie went back to her family farm and she showed and managed. She stayed in the amateur category.

She has a horse named Honey and still adores riding when she can. She loves to ride the trails.

Today, both sisters still professionally braid for shows.

It should be noted that sometime in the 1990s, Katharine Sanford left Sem after an illustrious career as Barn Manager. There was only praise for this wonderful woman. She was there for the riders and was always looking out for them. Such longevity and love deserves a round of applause, so wherever you are, stand up and give it to her.

She still lives in Rockbridge County and is married so now we call her Miss Sanford Connor. Bravo to you, Katharine. You made many a girl happy and gave them all confidence to be their best!

1991 Equitation Club
Image from the Seminary yearbook

The Virginia Horse Center

Adding to the excitement of what was going on in the Virginia horse scene in the 1980s, it was clear to the Lexington community that their town would be perfect for building a center where riders from all over could come and show. It would also become a huge economic boom to the town of Lexington and all surrounding areas of Virginia.

When approached with this idea, Governor Mills E. Godwin was very excited at the prospect. He formed a blue-ribbon commission to see just how viable this center could become. With town leaders and businessmen, especially, Otis Meade, and other town leaders, the project was heartily accepted and that meant it would become a reality.

None of this would go forward, however, without the help of certain other leaders in the equestrian world in Virginia and, once again, Southern Seminary would become the place to turn to. Russ Walther, who had been so successful raising money for the new barn for Sem, was now retired and living in Lexington, but they asked him to join the fundraising committee and also helped them with some tips on the course design.

In 1987, the plans were completed and they broke ground on 600 acres just north of Lexington, Virginia. This was to be a grand center where riders could come, show, board, and compete.

Today, the Virginia Horse Center has grown into a stunning place for riders, just as they had hoped. There is a 4,000 seat Coliseum, eight huge barns that can stable 1,000 horses, 11 show rings plus two very large indoor rings with parking on site and accommodations

Virginia Horse Center Entrance
Image courtesy of Carolyn Williams

Sem Memories

Virginia Horse Center nestled below the Blue Ridge Mountains
Image courtesy of Carolyn Williams

Katharine Sanford with Banner on her farm after his retirement
Image from the Seminary yearbook

close to the center.

At the dedication of the Center, Southern Seminary girls played host to all the dignitaries and guests who were invited. It was held at VMI and it was quite a special event.

Southern Sem student Felicia Guarino Phillips was chosen to be in their ads for the center and its on-going fundraising campaign.

The Virgina Horse Center is a beautiful place set beneath the magnificent Blue Ridge Mountains. You can find their schedule of events online at virginiahorsecenter.com

Dedication of the Horton-Ashway Horsemanship Center
Image from the Seminary yearbook

It Takes a Sisterhood

With all the incredible success stories on these pages, it takes a whole lot of people to get you to the top. In the history of Southern Seminary Jr. College, we see determination. It was, at times, a mentality akin to *The Little Engine That Could*. Determination to succeed in a shared vision is exactly what happened at Sem.

It began with one woman, who had a vision for young women to have a good education. Alice Chandler went from a small building in Bowling Green, Virginia to a very large, red building that still stands today in Buena Vista, Virginia. That building began as a hotel and then went on to become a wonderful, engaging, warm, and brilliant junior college under the loving hands of Margaret and Russell Robey.

In the seventies, Anne Mish, Director of the Physical Education Department, had hopes and dreams on expanding the equine program. She had a solid reputation in Virginia for equestrian excellence. She knew what had to be done to take the program that Cecil Stanford had overseen that was already at an excellent level to an even higher level, if she could get the right people to come as instructors. She made the calls and off she went to Mary Washington to talk to a man named Russ Walther. Russ's father had done well at that college teaching the girls there, but Miss Mish was able to talk Russ into going to Southern Seminary. He was keen on the idea and when he went and saw the facility, he knew he could do this. It was the end of the seventies now and Russ called the IHSA (Intercollegiate Horse Show Association) founder, Bob Cacchione, to go down to Southern Seminary and get them to join the Intercollegiate program. The IHSA was exactly what Sem needed to jump ahead in their program. They had excellent riders going to the school already and with this kind of competition, Sem would soar.

Bob Cacchione founded the Intercollegiate program in 1967 with the help of Jack Fritz, who knew all about how to form a vision and program as big as this. The concept was unique and would encompass riders of all levels and not be exclusive to anyone. They wanted young people to ride in competitions at all levels, regardless of their financial backgrounds, sex, race, religion or creeds. It was to become the one most important program for college students in America. Bob was eager to have Southern Seminary in the Eastern Division and after visiting and hearing about the Southern Seminary riders, Russ and Sem agreed this was the absolute necessary program to further advance the

Equine program at Sem.

Anne Mish worked with Russ Walther to make sure this opportunity would be a success and to have the riders prepared each year for the IHSA Team Competition.

None of them at that time could do more than dream of what might be in the school's future. When the program began to grow, the girls knew they would have to work and train harder than ever before to make the grade. They were already excellent riders but there were things to learn so they could ride at the highest level. That was the goal. Competition against other teams was going to be tough. They knew and were willing to do that, but they wanted to do this more than anything. And they did it!

The IHSA Competitions won under Russ Walther and JT Tallon are as follows:
- 1980 – team won
- 1981 – Grand Champions against St. Lawrence College
- 1982 – team won
- 1983 – team won
- 1984 – team won and that year, Beezie Patton won the Cacchione Cup won for individual excellence.
- 1985 – didn't win
- 1986 – team won

Under JT Tallon, the results were:
- 1987 – team won
- 1998 – team won

Words cannot fully describe how good these women were in competition. They were tough, determined, gutsy competitors, and yet fun-loving gals. Let's just say: WE ARE SEM PROUD!

Sem Whimsey

The Coffee Pot House
Image courtesy of Kipp Teague

Seminary Treasures
Image from a contributor

"For everything, there is a season..."
Ecclesiastes 3:1

I purposely did not write about the changing of the name of our alma mater (from Southern Seminary to Southern Sem) because I, personally, did not admire the decision. However, I understood the reason why and I guess if they felt that would save it from the inevitable, then so be it. I know how hard the decision must have been at that time, but when the name was changed, in the end, it would not matter at all. The name was just a part of what was changing everywhere. The world had changed and two-year colleges were facing hard decisions. Heartbreaking as it was for so many of us, the school was sold.

This author, now growing into her senior years, decided to keep those memories alive by writing books about the place we loved so much.

To write about the closing of the school was just too painful for most of us, but I do leave you with this thought: cherish our memories that we have and those I have written in my books. Make sure to reach out to your "Sem Sisters" whenever you can and keep them in your hearts forever.

Russ Walther, Holly Wallace, and Bob Cacchione
Image from a contributor

Acknowledgements

There are many people I would like to thank on the journey to finishing this story. It began with *The Ladies of the Seminary*, but I certainly couldn't end the adventure there. That was a fun and a rather wistful look back at the years we spent growing up and then where we all ended up.

This story, however, was always in my heart, because we all know that horses appeared on every ad that went out in the country about Southern Seminary so equestrians who wanted to get an education in equine arts, or take their horse to college with them, would be keen to go.

There was always excitement around a horse show the night before. To the riders, the barn was their "home away from home." Many have said they lovingly took on the name "Barn Rat" to identify themselves apart from the other girls. It really was appropriate as they spent as more time out there than anywhere else on campus.

In the beginning when I was totally dismayed at how to take a project of this size on and do it any justice at all, but I needed my "sisters." Holly Hill Wallace worked with me on many of things about the programs that were at Sem and she got me to Russ Walther who was an absolute Southern Gentleman in helping guide me along. My last stop was to speak with Bob Cacchione about this thing called IHSA.

After all that, I sat with so many Post-it notes stuck everywhere.

I got lucky when Holly told me, "You *have* to go to Ocala." My answer tells you all how totally unprepared I was when I asked her, "What's in Ocala?"

Well, off I went, and that's when it all began to come together and how I would go about this. I have to say I have never seen anything like that WEC in Ocala. It was incredible. I took it all in and watched the Grand Prix jumping competition. *Cool stuff*, I thought.

Holly had organized (beautifully) a reunion. Guess who showed up? Yep, Russ Walther and then Bob Cacchione walks in. *Wow*! I had hit the jackpot. Bob told the history of IHSA and told us how he got there. We all loved it and I was scribbling on every cocktail napkin in the room. When I left, I was still a bit wobbly about wring this all down for you, but I knew I really had to take it on. YOU ARE ALL TOO MARVELOUS NOT TO DO IT.

So, I thank Russ Walther, Bob Cacchione, Holly Hill Wallace and a special nod to Carolyn Hedrick Williams who has become such a good friend and a real Sem Sister along the way. How lucky so many of you were to have her teaching you. Carolyn was my go-to gal for information and I was off and running, texting back and forth with Carolyn sometimes several times a day. Thank you, thank you, Carolyn!

I finally met Miss Katharine Sanford Connor

who was, to me, the essence of the saying "still waters run deep." I could easily see why the young riders were so close to her.

I want to send a "thank you" to the Southern Virginia University archivist, Ethan, who helped us out immeasurably. And a kind word for all the staff of the Southern Virginia University who have graciously given us tours over the years and listened to our many stories of what it was like back then.

Several of the pictures in this journal were sent to me by Karen Leyers '84. I marveled at all of those pictures and realized nothing through the years at Sem had changed. I couldn't use them all, but thank you for sending them on.

This journal would never have seen the light of day without the intrepid team at Salt Water Media. I salute them with all my heart for their imagination, creativity, and complete professionalism. Thank you Stephanie Fowler, Patty Gregorio, and Andrew Heller.

Now done, I truly have to thank you ALL. In each conversation with many of you, I learned more and more things about your program and met so many wonderful Sem Sisters. We are an incredible sisterhood that will stand for as long as we live and even after the last alum passes on.

It's my hope that our spirits are still lingering around that grand old main building. The times I have been there, I would close my eyes and still hear the voices of all of us laughing, hurrying to get to the next class, or to the dining room. These are comforting memories.

I thank you all for sharing your pictures and recollections of your most beloved friends: your horses and other riders you were so close with at that time. Believe it or not, I actually fell in love with horses and those who rode them, more than I ever could have imagined.

Forgive me if there was an oversight or two. It was not on purpose. This was a massive job collecting and telling your stories and memories. But with all books, there are errors or omissions - never intentional, I can assure you.

Now, each time I pass a farm where the horses are out in the fields, I smile and say to myself, *I have met the greatest and the best girls who ride and teach and train and judge and jump and walk and canter and gallop thorough the air with love in their hearts for their horses. What now was a moment in time, we pause gently and think back, remembering how truly unbelievable those champions were - those Riders of the Seminary.*

**If you are looking
for one of these sisters
and need information,
I may be able to help.**

**Please reach out to me at
b.feldstein1234@gmail.com**

In Memory of
Kernan R. Hodges
Sem Sister from the late 1950s

Born in Franklin, Tennessee, Kernan loved horses all her life. She helped found the Middle Tennessee Pony Club, the first chartered by the United States Pony Club where Kernan was the first member to earn an "A" rating. Following her love of all things equine, she attended Southern Seminary. Afterward, she moved to Nashville, Tennessee where she continued teaching and helping others learn to love horses. Kernan married George Hodges and together they founded Deep Forest Stables. She spent her life dedicated to horses, riders, and the love of the industry.

Services

Below are listed just some of the services that our Sem Sisters offer to riders.

I know many who have profiles contained in this journal may not be listed because you may not have written me in time or missed the posting online. Deadlines are deadlines, darn it, but go back and checkout all the entries and see if there are any services you may be able to use. Our gals are everywhere, helping adults and kids to do amazing things with horses.

Here are some of the services that are offered from our Sem Sisters.

- Nancy Ginaven '59: Virginia Beach area- Horse Blanket Embroidery
- Nancy Dawn Ashway '72: Country Comfort Farm (owner) Boarding, Lessons, Indoor ring, Professional Judging - St. Michael's, MD
- Jo-Ann Greenbaum Schaudies '74: Poolesville, MD Breeds Champion Bassett Hounds
- Deb Hogue Hayes '74: Horse Boarding and teaching, Indian Trails, NC
- Barbara Ford '78: Virginia Beach Blackwater, Therapeutic Riding lessons and camps
- Terri Wherley '79: Hunter Glen Farm, Glen Rock, PA Sells hunter/jumpers
- Julie Whitlock McKee '80: Fox View Farm, Georgia, Breeds, Buys and Sells
- Lori Wright Lehman '83: East Berlin,Pa. Tack Room Treasures Consignment tack, New and used for riders
- Renee Birchell '83: Equibalance PEMF magnetic therapy for horses and their hearts
- Tracy Scott '85: Skyland Farms, Kentucky- retirement home for horses
- Patty Messina '88: Ocala, Florida Riding lessons and horse sales
- Tamara (Tammy) Ginaven Robbins '88: Equine Logos

Tackroom Treasures by Lori Wright Lehman '83
Image courtesy of Lori Lehman

Praise for Southern Seminary

"In 1982, I arrived at Southern Sem to be the Director of Student Counseling and then in 1984 became the Dean of students. I was blessed to be there during the most exciting years of the equestrian program. I didn't have any exposure to horses prior to so it was a steep learning curve for me. I somewhat oversaw the budgets of the equine program and with no experience, I had to move quickly to understand the costs of hay and footing and have to say I was shocked at the vet and shoeing bills. I relied heavily on the expertise of the Athletic Director, Anne Mish. I lived close to the barn and quickly became acquainted with my equine neighbors. Sem riders had assets upon their arrival that set them apart from the other students. Years of training provided them with discipline, a sense of comradery, poise beyond their years and independence. I came to know many of the riders very well and stay in touch with many of them today. I am awed by their impressive careers both in and out of the horse industry."

"One Quick story that I must tell is about the November, 4th 1985 flood that hit Buena Vista. It came after a large mixer the student council hosted for the girls, faculty, their parents, the VMI cadets and W&L fellows. It was held in the barn which was the only place that was big enough to accommodate such an affair with room for eating, dancing, and a live band. Hay bales served as seating for the guests. When it was over and the guests had gone home or to morels for the night, the waters came rushing down the hillsides and into the small town. Everyone was taken by surprise and trapped. No way in or out. The Maury Bridge was closed, the town was in trouble. That is when the Sem gals got going. A bucket brigade went from the swimming pool to Main in order to flush toilets. Town folks brought their cars up and parked them on Sem Hill. A sparse kitchen staff made sandwiches and whatever they could find to feed the people coming on campus for help. A disaster relief station was set up and the girls gave out needed items to folks that were totally stranded. However, I must say I was astonished at the Sem riders who stayed to care for their horses. I will never forget the display of courage of these young women."

— Paula Sherlock
Kentucky, Family Court Judge (Ret.)
Dean of Students